Norman

Best wishes

Viv Lawson

Régina Diana

Régina Diana

Seductress, Singer, Spy

Vivien Newman
and
David Semeraro

First published in Great Britain in 2017 by
Pen & Sword History
an imprint of
Pen & Sword Books Ltd
47 Church Street
Barnsley
South Yorkshire
S70 2AS

ISBN 978 1 47386 150 3

A CIP catalogue record for this book is available from the British Library.

Printed and bound in England
by TJ International Ltd.

Pen & Sword Books Ltd incorporates the Imprints of Pen & Sword Books Archaeology, Atlas, Aviation, Battleground, Discovery, Family History, History, Maritime, Military, Naval, Politics, Railways, Select, Transport, True Crime, Fiction, Frontline Books, Leo Cooper, Praetorian Press, Seaforth Publishing, Wharncliffe and White Owl.

For a complete list of Pen & Sword titles please contact
PEN & SWORD BOOKS LIMITED
47 Church Street, Barnsley, South Yorkshire, S70 2AS, England
E-mail: enquiries@pen-and-sword.co.uk
Website: www.pen-and-sword.co.uk

(Vivien Newman)

This book is for my husband Ivan, constant companion, occasional devil's advocate and always wise counsellor. He willingly ferried two lost souls around 'Kilometre 0' and patiently pointed out whether we were in 1914–1918 France, Germany or Switzerland. It is also for my sister Lucinda Semeraro whose enthusiasm for this project led her to embark not only on the 10km circuit 'Kilometre 0', but also to stay in the only area of France which is a 'food-free' zone.

(David Semeraro)

This book is for my grandfather (Grandy) Earle Raymond Adler 1914–1994. It is my way of thanking him for the inexhaustible curiosity he instilled in me. It is also for my sons; may the passion of what you believe in, make you overcome all odds.

Contents

Acknowledgements

(Vivien Newman)

First and foremost, my nephew and now co-author, David Semeraro. Without his insistence, I would have abandoned the quest for the 'Swiss singer Régina Diane'.

Once again, several friends have patiently listened to my ideas, thoughts and theories and allowed me to test these, and accept or finally reject them. In particular:

Professor Pam Cox who, years ago, made me realise that 'bad girls' can be so much more interesting than good ones!

Keith Dolan, ever my Great War sounding block, this time for ideas and advice about Marseille's crucial role in troop transportation.

Warrant Officer Christopher Earl and his detailed information about shooting skills, positions, rounds per minute and accuracy.

Michaela Lamb, my 'spin class buddy', and Clare Russell, my power walking one, whose early interest in and enthusiasm for Régina and her story never seemed to wane despite the hundreds of miles we must have covered since I (and they!) first heard of her.

Monique Serneels and Maria Weiss, my Swiss friends of many decades, my daughters' godmothers and mothers of my goddaughters. Through them I learnt to love Switzerland and see beyond its cuckoo clocks, chocolate and pure mountain air. Also Dr Christiane Furrer, who so efficiently sourced articles via the University of Lausanne library's e-resources when JSTOR let me down.

Last but by no means least, my daughters Rosalind and Elizabeth, who still indulge their 'funny mummy' and always ask 'how's the book going?' – and, I think, listen to the reply.

(David Semeraro)

I would like to express my deepest appreciation to all those who have enabled me to complete this book.

Especial gratitude to:

My wife, for putting up with this 'ménage à trois' and for going along with this long-lasting and time-consuming obsession, and my boys, for putting up with a busy daddy.

Furthermore, I would also like to acknowledge and express appreciation for their crucial contributions to:

Gaspard Grass, Geneva, former History teacher now retired, who showed me how to access the Archives de Genève and bypass some of the paperwork.

Aurélien Grass, his son and my mate, Military Medic, Geneva, for his tolerance towards a somewhat distracted colleague.

Emmanuel Ducry, Archives de Genève, who graciously gave permission to use all the materials needed to complete our task.

A special thanks to Mélanie Fournier of the Department Fédéral de l'Intérieur, who helped me begin this journey down the murky paths of forgotten history.

Last but not least, many thanks go to the head of the project and co-author, Dr Vivien Newman, my aunt, who so innocently triggered my curiosity and sent me on this crazy crusade through murk and mystery, and for her drive in guiding me in achieving this goal.

And to any others who I may have forgotten to name, may they find here a sincere token of gratitude.

Both authors would like to express their gratitude to Karyn Burnham for her careful editing and useful comments. Any faults that remain are of course our own.

Chapter 1

Who WAS Régina Diana?

My first interest in Régina Diana was sparked in early 2013. I was in the middle of writing *We Also Served: The Forgotten Women of the First World War* and was researching the spy Mata Hari. Flicking through the contemporary *The War Illustrated*, which gave subscribers a rather unbalanced view of the war as it unfolded, I noticed on 17 November 1917 a multi-photograph spread entitled 'Agents of Prussia's World-Wide Espionage'. Adjacent to the picture of Mata Hari 'the celebrated Hindu dancer', was another, equally grainy, image. The caption informed readers this was 'Régina Diane [sic], a Swiss singer who had been condemned to death in France on being found guilty as a German spy'. Having been brought up in the Swiss city of Lausanne, I was immediately intrigued. Despite my early love of history and interest in the Great War, I had never heard of a Swiss singer/spy. Who was she? A quick search of the internet would surely resolve this question – or so I thought. Instead, a lengthy search produced two miniscule 'hits' from an Australian newspaper site but beyond the supplementary information that 'Régina Diana' had been condemned to death at Marseille and had, by 7 January 1918, been shot, there was little to add to *The War Illustrated* one-sentence teaser.

Musing over this Marseille execution, I remembered having read the diary of Nursing Sister Burgess held at the Peter Liddle Archive. Referring to Marseille in December 1917, she had asserted, 'the town is full of spies' and that sisters were only allowed out in 'twos or threes during the day or in fours or sixes at night.' Having initially dismissed this as the spy fever that was prevalent throughout the war in England, France, Germany, and, as I would eventually discover, neutral Switzerland, I had thought little of it. But, was Sister Burgess maybe referring to Régina Diana? Despite the press restrictions about reporting spying, was news of her trial and its verdict common knowledge in Marseille?

I contacted my sister, an English teacher still living near Lausanne. Perhaps she could try to track down elusive Régina Diana via a former student, a journalist for a Lausanne newspaper. She held out little hope but, used to strange requests from her history-obsessed sibling, she agreed to see what she could discover – which, despite her best efforts, turned out to be strictly nothing. She mentioned Régina to her son David, my 'Swiss' nephew and now co-author, and it was as though he had been hit by a lightning bolt. We HAD to find her. Undeterred by my comment that, however determined the researcher, sometimes the past will not give up its secrets, this, he announced, was one secret he and I were going to uncover. We spent hours on various newspaper archive sites and got excited whenever we got a 'hit' with the search term 'Swiss spy', but the excitement turned to frustration as the spy was never 'Régina Diana'. We tried putting requests for information on numerous English and French Great War related forums but again to little avail.

Next we emailed the City of Marseille archives. Eventually they replied – they had no information. They suggested we contact the Service Historique de la Défense (SHD) in Paris – who only respond (slowly) to written as opposed to electronic requests for information. Eventually, some six or seven months into the quest, they replied. Having expected the written equivalent of the famous Gallic shrug, I opened the letter slightly half-heartedly. To my amazement, they confirmed that a spy with the alias Régina Diana had indeed faced a firing squad in Marseille in January 1918; they provided the additional information that her real name was Marie-Antoinette Avvico and that she was not a Swiss national but had been resident in Geneva all her life (I have since discovered that if the war had broken out only a few weeks later, she would have been granted Swiss nationality and the outcome to her story may have been very different). They even helpfully provided reference numbers for the papers held at the French Military archives at the Chateau de Vincennes in Paris where documents can be consulted by those holding a reader's pass. Surprisingly for French bureaucracy, these seemed relatively easy to acquire as long as one presented oneself with all the correct paperwork and evidence of need. We were getting somewhere, or so we thought. David and I agreed to meet in Paris, spend a day jointly going through the Avvico files and there would just be time to squeeze a couple of paragraphs about her into *We Also Served* then she and – at least from my point of view – my nephew, would leave me in peace.

At Vincennes, with our shiny new readers' passes clutched in our hands, we were directed towards our allocated seats and waited for the pre-ordered documents to surface. David grinned like a Cheshire cat as our names were called and we were presented with two weighty boxes. We opened them and hundreds of dusty papers tumbled out. BUT these related to relatively minor military offences committed by poilus in the Northern French départements (roughly equivalent to British counties) of Oise (60) and Somme (80) in 1915; 'drunk and disorderly' was the most common misdemeanour. Sentences consisted of a couple of days in the guardhouse. There was the occasional more serious offence, but no sign of a spy or an execution. We started thumbing through quickly, desperately searching for information relating to the Southern French Bouches du Rhone département (13) in which Marseille is situated, preferably for 1917. Maybe the papers we needed would be hidden somewhere.

It began to dawn on us that we had got the wrong boxes. I checked against my letter from the SHD and the numbers we had ordered – they tallied. The reference numbers, not the boxes, were incorrect. As these are military archives, the reading room is run along military lines, or so it seemed to my untutored eyes; our request to speak to an official who might be able to help had to go through various levels of the military hierarchy and, this being France, the reading room closed for lunch. David had to return to Switzerland that evening and I to Chelmsford, time was not on our side. Eventually, the officer in charge agreed to listen to our query. Initially we were met with an adamant 'Non!' No one could help us to find even the correct references and certainly, even if we found them, the boxes would not be available for at least 48 hours. Then a young NCO who had been listening to our pleas, stood to attention, threw a crisp salute and having been given permission to speak, whispered in the ear of 'Mon Capitaine'. Having resisted the temptation to return the salute (as a military medic I am sure David would have done the Swiss Army proud), we stood up tall and smiled hopefully – maybe we were getting somewhere. 'Mon Capitaine' promised to see what he could do. He suggested we went to have lunch and he kindly wished us 'Bon Appétit' – his face suggested he would have preferred 'Bon Voyage'!

Sitting in a restaurant near to the Chateau de Vincennes, then unbeknownst to us at the very site where Régina herself may have had a coffee when she was in Paris spying on this self-same Chateau de Vincennes, we 'brainstormed' why she might have been in Marseille. We produced a long list of reasonable-sounding ideas, and, suitably fortified by lunch, we returned to the fray to test our ideas against the contents of the files that we were hopeful now awaited us.

Back in the hushed atmosphere of the reading room, 'Mon Capitaine' summoned us to an inner sanctum where his leather-topped desk was located – not a computer in sight. He regretted to inform us that the papers could not currently be examined. He announced in a whisper that all files held on people who had been executed by the French Army during the war were being digitised; the project would be completed in November 2014 – the month my book was being published. Only then would the documents be available for public consultation. I began remonstrating. Surely this little rule could be bent for 24 hours which we thought would be long enough either to get the gist of her story or at least copy the documents. By now heartily sick of these representatives from perfidious Albion and supposedly neutral Switzerland, he took a fountain pen out of his pocket and, having located a piece of blotting paper and carefully wiped the nib, he wrote down an address – not an email but a postal one. We were instructed to write to a certain colonel who may be able to give dispensation for us to view the files but almost certainly wouldn't – on no account were we to disclose who had given us the colonel's name.

Having all but signed a confidentiality agreement, we decided I would write a begging letter to the colonel. (Whether we ever got an answer, I cannot now remember but I think not). In any case, it was obvious that it would be too late to include Régina in *We Also Served*, although I made reference to her. It seemed we would have to remain patient until the Mémoire des Hommes website went live in November 2014, at that point maybe I could place an article about her somewhere. She slipped to the back of my mind as other projects and books materialised. Then in November, I got an email from David. The site was up and running and there was indeed a database of Great War executions. He had entered her name into the search box and multiple documents had appeared. He phoned a few days later, his excitement was audible. 'It's an amazing story; there are pages and pages of information, photographs and the whole of the court case. We've GOT to do something with it.'

'Doing something with it' has taken us both on a long physical and metaphorical journey, one that we would never have anticipated on that February day in 2014. It is a story which needs to be set in the context in which it unfolded: a context which encompasses the history of female spies, the crises surrounding Swiss neutrality, skilled and ruthless spy handlers, the seedy world of café concert, lusty French patriotic songs and the troubled wartime history of the city of Marseille situated deep in the South of France far from the fighting fronts. All played their part in turning Marie-Antoinette Avvico into Régina Diana and leading her towards the 'Champ de Tir du Pharo' one early January morning in 1918.

(Vivien Newman)

An Unexpected Journey

Little did I know after hanging up the telephone following a brief conversation with my mother, that my life was about to change, profoundly. Little did

I expect to be literally obsessed by an obscure woman shot for high treason a century ago. Little did I anticipate the dedication I would muster and that she would become part of my everyday life for over three years. And nothing could have prepared me for taking part in writing a book – and even writing it in English. Although half British, French is my first language and, far from being either an historian or an author, I am a Swiss Army medic.

The request my mother had relayed was, or so it seemed then, quite simple. 'Can you try and find information concerning a Swiss female spy shot during the Great War.' This plea came from my Aunt, Dr Vivien Newman, a renowned specialist in women's often forgotten contributions to the First World War. Being a Swiss resident, my geographical proximity to the source of information seemed to make her request a reasonable one, particularly as she knew I had always loved history. This love was about to become an obsession.

I could never have guessed the ramifications of that simple phone call. Initially, I too turned to the internet. I entered the words: Woman Spy, Shot, 1918 into my browser, all that came back was Mata-Hari. Thousands of results for her but not a trace of the woman I was after. Not the slightest hint. Nothing! An unknown warrior…

I turned to the Archives de la Confédération Helvétique who were unable even to confirm whether Régina Diane (as we then called her) was Swiss. No record mentioned her, let alone provided any information relating to where she came from and where she had lived. One could have expected that if a Swiss national had been shot by France, there would be some trace of her. It was not to be. She was nowhere to be found…

Perhaps the real reason that I have become so intrigued is because I feel that History has been unfair to Régina Diana and I have always hated injustices. It has often been noted that history being written by the victors, spies are divided into categories those who spied for 'our side' are 'good', those working for the enemy, 'bad'. But human beings and their actions are more complex. And as you are about to discover, the path along which this 'enemy' spy travelled was a fraught one. Why she chose to embark on it we can finally only surmise, but I hope that by the time you have finished reading her story you will agree that Régina Diana was an outstanding agent, despite most certainly not fighting on 'our' side.

(David Semeraro)

We both hope you will find this story as fascinating to read as we have found it to uncover.

Chapter 2

'The Second Oldest Profession'

Exactly 366 days after America entered the war, *The* (New York) *Sun*, 7 April 1918, offered readers a dramatic illustrated spread: 'Queens of the Spy World Whose Intrigues Sway the Fate of Nations'. The article's sensational title and contents were light years away from the 1899 Hague Convention's attempts to define and codify multiple aspects of 'war on land and sea' including spying which, as both the Convention delegates and *The Sun* journalist conceded, is integral to warfare. Chapter II 'On Spies', both recognized the omnipresence of intelligence and gave spies protection in law:

> *An individual can only be considered a spy if, acting clandestinely, or on false pretences, he obtains, or seeks to obtain information in the zone of operations of a belligerent, with the intention of communicating it to the hostile party.* (Article 29)

Furthermore,

> *A spy taken in the act cannot be punished without previous trial.* (Article 30)

Far removed from the dry language of the Convention, lurid, melodramatic spy novels and supposedly eye-witness accounts penned by those caught up in this murky underworld, gripped late nineteenth and early twentieth century readers, reaching their apotheosis during the so-called Great War for European Civilization. Melodramatic accounts of dastardly undercover wartime agents filled many newspaper columns, even neutral ones, although the veracity of the tales may not always stand up to scrutiny.

Aware of its readers' seemingly insatiable appetite for spy material, on 8 June 1916 the widely-read francophone Swiss newspaper, *La Gazette de Lausanne* had published sixteen definitions of the word 'spy' gleaned from the writings of famous nineteenth century men (no woman's contribution appeared). Amongst these, William Gladstone believed only 'despotic governments and tyrants' would surround themselves with spies, the Count of Cavour preferred 'defeat than a victory achieved through the assistance of spies', whilst Gustave Modena claimed spies represented the 'lowest point' to which humanity could stoop. Lowest point or not, spies have existed ever since mankind has sought military or commercial advantage over his fellows, with women as well as men deeply involved. In his classic fifth Century BC *The Art of War,* Sun Tzu devotes a whole chapter to 'The Use of Spies', concluding: 'Spies are a most important element in war'; they are the 'sovereign's most precious faculty'. Sun Tzu acknowledges that spies come with a price to pay but to 'grudge the outlay of a hundred ounces of silver in honours and emoluments is the height of inhumanity'.

In times and geographical locations nearer to our own than Sun Tzu's China, references to spies abound. Doctoral candidate Bertrand Warusfel notes how as the 'nation state' became more firmly established in sixteenth to eighteenth century Europe, the 'practice of secrecy' became increasingly formalised, with bureaux developing to handle both the spies and the information they gathered.

Although The Hague Convention articles assume that spies will be masculine, a whistle-stop tour through spying in the so-called 'Modern Era' (c.1500 onwards) demonstrates that intelligence gathering has never been an exclusively male preserve. Régina and her fellow Great War spies were far from the first of their gender to supply their (pay)masters with crucial information. Women from very diverse backgrounds have left a significant mark on what is sometimes referred to as the 'second oldest profession'.

(A very few) Female spies in history

Sixteenth century Queen Elizabeth I's Secretary of State, Sir Francis Walsingham, aware of the plots and intrigues surrounding the monarch, established a network of around fifty spies; believing women's 'invisibility' rendered them ideal for espionage work, some were female. In her doctoral thesis, Hsuan-Ying Tu argues that women played an important role in 'information management as gatherers, readers, purveyors and writers of news and as spymasters'. Their unique access to the monarch enabled them to relay credible information about England's 'capricious Queen'. Eager to foster intelligence gathering about Elizabeth (Spain's greatest enemy), the Spanish Ambassador cultivated pre-established contacts with Elizabeth Parr, first Marchioness of Northampton who was 'in favour with the Queen and has served His Majesty [Philip II] when opportunity has occurred'. The queen herself was playing a similar game; she used her women of the Chamber to supply her with intelligence from foreign courts. Although not providing wartime intelligence, several of these female 'chamberers' were relaying and receiving information both to and from external sources sometimes in the queen's favour, sometimes, dangerously, working against it.

Elizabeth Stuart, Queen of Bohemia 1596–1662

If the female spy ring surrounding Elizabeth I remains largely anonymous, more is known about her kinswoman and goddaughter, Elizabeth Stuart, sister to England's ill-fated King Charles I. Dubbed the Winter Queen, she was a skilled linguist who even as a child was a copious letter writer. Married at the age of 17 to Frederick V, Count Palatine of the Rhine, leader of the Protestant rulers in Germany, she rapidly became the marriage's dominant partner. Nadine Akkerman has scrutinised letters sent by Elizabeth following the couple's 1621 exile in The Hague. Whilst those she sent through official channels were anodyne, those dispatched via Antwerp and Brussels contained secret codes and invisible ink as she sought (unsuccessfully) to rally support from diplomats, members of the clergy, and powerful Protestant rulers, for her husband's return to his lost throne. She wrote hundreds of letters in cipher code, employing at least seven keys during her lifetime, encrypting her letters herself with hieroglyphics and the use of multiple alphabets to avoid the prying eyes of those who continued to plot against her husband. For Lisa Jardine, Elizabeth's 'lobbying, bargaining, negotiating and cajoling', not to mention her cryptographic skills, 'made her a major player during a particularly unsettled period of European history.'

Akkerman argues that far from Elizabeth's involvement in espionage being unique in this period, there were 'at least sixty female spies in overlapping networks'. Payment books for the English Secret Service included the names of many women – although 'Secret Service' could be an agent's euphemism for a visit to a prostitute. Sometimes described as 'adventuresses' or even as 'Royalist heroines', these women were, like the spies who would walk in their footsteps between 1914 and 1918, drawn from all ranks of society: nurses, shopkeepers, actresses, noble women, even a playwright, they shared a similarity – they could, in modern terminology, 'slip beneath the radar'. Being female, they could move about without anyone noticing or suspecting them. Régina, as we shall see, was constantly, seemingly innocently, on the move.

Aphra Behn (1640–1689)

Aphra Behn is renowned for being among the earliest female English playwrights. Her 'other' career is far less well known. A (possible) short-lived marriage to a Mr Behn, a merchant of Dutch extraction living in London who died in 1665, provided her with distinct advantages for the widowed Aphra spoke Dutch as well as English, and England and Holland had been sporadically at war for several years. Noticed by Lord Arlington, head of Charles II's Intelligence Office, given the alias 'Astrea', or Agent 160, she was sent to visit an English political exile in Antwerp to acquire intelligence relating to Dutch plans to invade England. In her quest, 'Astrea' accumulated debts amounting to £150 (around £20,500 in 2016); her pleas for reimbursement were rejected. Worse in terms of national security, arguably because she was female, the coded, detailed letters she sent to England regarding the proposed Dutch invasion were erroneously dismissed; Régina's spymaster did not reproduce similar errors 250 years later. In 1667, the Dutch sailed up the Thames, captured the flagship the *Royal Charles* and took her back to Amsterdam; her metal stern piece showing the English Coat of Arms is now exhibited in the Rijksmuseum.

Anna 'Nancy' Strong (1740–1812)

Just over a century later, England was at war with her American colonies. According to the American National Women's History Museum, 'spy networks sprang up throughout the colonies', providing critical intelligence and 'many undercover agents were women'. Some women successfully infiltrated enemy lines, often acting as pedlars selling useful items to soldiers. Inside the camp, they kept their eyes peeled and ears to the ground to gain information about troops, artillery and provisions – information that spies in the Great War, including Régina, would, in their turn, be asked to provide, irrespective for whose side they were spying.

Spies frequently operate in rings and the most elaborate network centred around New York; intelligence was passed through many (often female) hands. On the surface, there might have been little to make anyone think twice about Mrs Anna Strong. Her nine children would surely have kept her busy with domestic chores. Outward appearances can be deceptive and along with washing, shopping and cooking, she was sending coded messages and signals to other agents in the anti-British Culper Spy Ring. Boatmen picked up and delivered messages across the Long Island Sound which the British had controlled since 1776, thus a perilous undertaking. Despite the British becoming suspicious and probably occupying Anna's property, they were unable to see what, or whom, was staring them in the face. She was simply using her washing line to conceal messages – a black petticoat would announce an agent's arrival and handkerchiefs pegged in a certain order revealed at which of six locations a boat was moored which could be used to deliver information to George Washington's Headquarters. The under-valuing of women's abilities and worth, not to mention the domestic nature of her coded intelligence, enabled her ring to flourish. The contemporary male military minds could not envision a woman being deeply involved in espionage; the officers were simply outwitted by a black petticoat and coloured hankies fluttering in the breeze. Today, one New York chapter of the Daughters of the American Revolution is known as the Anna Strong Chapter; their insignia, a petticoat and handkerchiefs, commemorates her washing-line.

Elizabeth Van Lew (1818–1900) and Mary Bowser (precise dates unknown, b. around 1839)

Six decades later, during the American Civil War, female spies again proliferated and initially the same male mind-set prevailed: women were innocent and unthreatening, an attitude which altered as commanders on both sides realised that, far from being above suspicion, women were often at the heart of intelligence gathering. This changing attitude increased the risks for those involved.

Born into a socially privileged family in Richmond, Virginia, Elizabeth Van Lew's abolitionist sentiments culminated in her family's freeing their nine slaves in 1843. Nineteen years later, on April 17 1862, much to 44-year-old Elizabeth's distress, the Virginia Convention voted to leave the Union (Northern States) and throw in its lot with the Confederate (slave-owning Southern) States; Richmond, her home town, became the Confederacy's capital in the bitter Civil War.

Elizabeth Van Lew secretly began to work for the Union. Using the pretext of taking small comforts to internees, she was, to the horror of her social peers, permitted to start visiting the prison camp in Richmond where Union PoWs were held. Whilst distributing gifts, she gleaned what information she could from prisoners, subsequently helping some to escape. Recruited by the Union, she began operating a spy ring (which included twelve female agents) at the very heart of the Confederacy. Instructed, as Régina would be, in how to send information in coded messages, she proved a quick learner as well as a fast thinker; she kept the cipher in the case of her watch and took the additional precaution of often sending reports, including military intelligence, in invisible ink. Her family's former slaves were sometimes used to carry and drop messages concealed in a shoe, sewn into a garment, or buried in a hollowed-out egg, in a series of 'safe houses'. What sets her apart is how, exploiting both misogyny and racial prejudice, she penetrated to the very heart of the 'White House of the Confederacy' in Richmond, which served both as Confederate President Jefferson Davis's home and his executive office.

Her family's former slaves included a young girl called Mary whose (illegal) education Elizabeth had almost certainly funded. In late 1862 or 1863, by placing Mary as a 'slave' within the inner sanctum, Elizabeth infiltrated the Confederate White House. Trebly invisible due to her gender, her slave status and her race, Mary became privy to information intended only for Jefferson Davis. He and his entourage saw no need to guard their tongues within the safe confines of the 'White House' and they had no scruples about leaving secret documents around. If they had thought about her, or indeed even noticed her, they would have assumed that, in conformity with the slave laws of the time, Mary was illiterate. Instead she was busy acquiring and storing sensitive information in her photographic memory. This she relayed, via a seamstress and a local baker, to Elizabeth. The baker subsequently remembered how 'Everything Mary saw on the Rebel President's desk, she could repeat word for word'.

George H. Sharpe, Intelligence Officer for the Army of the Potomac and General Grant, credited Elizabeth's ring as being responsible for 'the greater portion of our intelligence in 1864–1865'. Following the North's victory, General, now President, Ulysses S. Grant appointed her Postmistress of Richmond, the highest federal post open to a woman. The Richmond newspapers were unimpressed, the appointment 'of a Federal spy' was a 'deliberate insult to our people.' No prestigious appointment went to Mary Bowser, whose contribution to the Van Lew network, and indeed to the Union victory, has only recently been reassessed; 130 years after the cessation of hostilities, the American Military Intelligence Hall of Fame at Fort Huachuca, Arizona, honoured her memory:

> *Ms. Bowser certainly succeeded in a highly dangerous mission to the great benefit of the Union effort. She was one of the highest placed and most productive espionage agents of the Civil War.*

Rose Greenhow (1813/14–1864)

Credited by some historians with playing a key part in the Confederate States' early victory at the July 1861 Battle of Bull Run, Rose O'Neal

Greenhow believed passionately in the rightness of the South's cause. An ambitious socialite, friendships with powerful and influential members of Washington's élite, particularly senators from the South, led her to espouse the South's cause. Spying brought her into contact with President Jefferson Davis – as friend not foe.

In 1861, Rose lived in Washington, sixty miles from the Mason-Dixon line which divided the Union from the Confederacy. Although capital of the Northern states, Washington was full of Southern sympathisers. However, despite Rose's well-known pro-South leanings, she entertained Northern Army officers in her central Washington home. A careful listener (as Régina would become), Rose took note of all the military and political chatter surrounding her. Undoubtedly, the high-ranking gentlemen at her table would have discounted a mere female's ability to follow tactical conversations. Little did they realise that their elegant hostess was forwarding information to the Southern Rebels across the Potomac and Rappahannock rivers. Recruited by a former officer in the US Army, now aide-de-camp to the Southern General Pierre G. T. Beauregard, who had foreseen Rose's usefulness as a spy, he taught her the rudiments of cryptography. However, his failure to instil in her the need for ultra-caution when handling information, and the importance of destroying evidence, would have disastrous consequences. She was neither the first nor the last spy to be caught due to lack of caution. Such a momentary lapse of caution, coupled with bad luck, sealed the fate of many spies, including Régina.

In early July 1861 Rose was determined to alert Southern commanders of the Union's intentions to move on the Confederates at Manassas in (Confederate) Virginia. Aware that voluminous skirts and elaborate hairstyles are hiding places a chivalrous man would never dream of investigating, she had included several young women in her spy ring. They slipped in and out of farms, taverns and waterfront docks, mingling with the melting pot of humanity that congregated in such places, the very same world that Régina would be familiar with fifty-five years later. Placing the message in a tiny black silk purse, Rose instructed a young courier to wind it up in her hair. An aide noted how, on arrival at General Beauregard's HQ near Fairfax County Courthouse,

> *She took out her tucking comb and let fall the longest and most beautiful roll of hair I have ever seen. She took then from the back of her head, where it had been safely tied, a small package, not larger than a silver dollar, sewed up in silk.*

The package's ten words of vital information were also passed to Confederate President Jefferson Davis. While some historians argue that the intelligence was far from crucial and that it was Confederate tactics and Union errors which swayed the outcome, others agree with Davis (and, unsurprisingly Rose herself) that her message was a deciding factor in the First Battle of Bull Run's victorious outcome for Beauregard and the South.

Whatever Rose's contribution, her fate was sealed when Union troops overran the Fairfax Courthouse: papers and maps incriminating her were found. Head of the US Intelligence Service, Glasgow-born Allan Pinkerton, now had her firmly in his sights and, as would happen with Régina, he waited to move against her until he had amassed sufficient evidence. In late August 1861, she was charged with 'being a spy in the interest of the rebels and furnishing the insurgent generals with important information relative to the movements of the Union forces'.

Rose's lack of training in the finer details of spy-craft contributed to her downfall. Although she tried to burn these when Pinkerton closed in on her, singed scraps of paper revealed notes on military movements and encoded messages with copies of the code. Initially placed under house arrest, she short-sightedly assured Pinkerton that given half a chance, she would kill him. She continued to communicate with her handler Jordan, thereby fuelling the case against her although, as the Confederates knew she was compromised, it is doubtful whether they trusted any of her information. She tried to hoodwink Pinkerton's agents by leaving around a bottle of invisible ink, hoping to convince those intercepting her correspondence that they should check for invisible writing as opposed to coded, seemingly innocent messages, generally of a suitable feminine nature – for example one referred to children's shoes.

In December, she was imprisoned in the Old Capital Prison, now the site of the US Supreme Court Building. To her chagrin, she did not feel that those imprisoned with her were her social equals, nor were the living conditions to her taste! The *Semi Weekly State Journal (Raleigh, North Carolina 7 June 1862)* agreed with her, her 'privations were enough to wring the stoutest heart'. However, the 19 January *Philadelphia Press* saw her more prosaically as a 'female traitor' but stressed that her accommodation, which she shared with her young daughter, whilst not luxurious, was comfortable.

In March 1862, as a first step in determining whether she should stand trial she was given a hearing. Despite the weight of damning evidence which had been painstaking accumulated, President Lincoln refrained from taking this step. The inevitable 'guilty' verdict would culminate in the penalty 'death by hanging'. Unlike both his German and French counterparts half a century later, he was reluctant to execute a woman, particularly one of Rose's social standing, an act which would provide the South with a martyr. Better to deport her to the Confederacy where she renewed her acquaintance with Confederate President Jefferson Davis. During their subsequent meetings in the Richmond White House, did she ever notice, a black slave whose name was Mary Bowser?

Travelling through England and France, carrying dispatches promoting the Southern States' cause, she met with the highest echelons of British and French society and published her memoir, *My Imprisonment and the First Year of Abolition Rule at Washingto*n. Carrying secret dispatches for the South, she returned home aboard southern blockade-runner *Condor;* the ship ran into difficulties on 1 October 1864 off the coast of North Carolina. Afraid of being re-captured by the North, Rose made an ill-fated bid for shore. Allegedly weighted down by royalty money, which she had sown into her clothes, she was drowned. Washed ashore, she was given a funeral with full military honours. Major William Doster, the provost marshal who provided security for Washington, considered her to be 'formidable', an agent with 'masterly skill,' who bestowed on the Confederacy 'her knowledge of all the forces which reigned at the Capitol'. Her grave commemorates 'Mrs Rose O'Neal Greenhow: A Bearer of Dispatches to the Confederate Government'. This strong, determined woman who used both her feminine charms and her iron will, is still honoured for her significant contribution to the Confederate Cause.

Juliette Dodu (1848–1909)

In 1870, the winds of war embroiled France and the independent German states (Prussia being the dominant force) resulting in the humiliating loss of the French provinces of Alsace and much of Lorraine. This scarred France for a generation and would have an impact on the way soldiers from Marseille who were accused of lacking military fervour, were viewed by the French High Command during the First World War. Decades later, French spy Louise Thuliez wrote:

> *The memory of the Franco-Prussian War was still fresh in every heart. We children heard frequent allusion to Alsace and Lorraine; our maps marked the lost provinces in black.*

One would expect to find stories of at least a few female spies during this catastrophic war. Although one woman was decorated by France, historians now cast doubt on the tale. With no other contender for the role of female spy in this war however, her story is worth telling.

Born in the French Indian Ocean territory of La Réunion, Juliette Dodu was 2 when her French Navy surgeon father died. In 1864, she and her mother came to France and worked in the Pithviers telegraph office in Loiret. Six years later, the Prussian invaders occupied Pithviers just before the fall of Sédan on 1 September 1870. The telegraph wires were cut and the Dodus was forced to live 'above the shop'. Apparently, Juliette rigged up a tap on the wires that passed through her bedroom, intercepting Morse code transmissions sent along the wires by the Prussians, allegedly saving thousands of French lives. Some witnesses claim that she did this for three weeks until her stratagem was uncovered and the occupiers realised that this outwardly charming young woman was communicating their secrets to the French High Command. Court-martialled, she was sentenced to death, but the signing of an Armistice between the belligerents led to her reprieve.

In 1873 Juliette met the owner of *Le Figaro* newspaper. Four years later, the first account of the 'Legend of Dodu' appeared; on 30 July 1878, she became the first woman to receive the Cross of the Légion d'Honneur and Military Medal. The decree, signed by Maréchal de France, Patrice de MacMahon, stated that she was being decorated for her interception of 'dispatches at the peril of her life, for being condemned to death by the enemy, and saved only by the cessation of hostilities'. She died near Montreux in Switzerland in 1909. Her body was repatriated with significant pomp and ceremony. Having lain in state for two days, she was accorded a national funeral and buried at Paris' famous Cimetière Père Lachaise.

Yet questions had already been posed over the account's reliability – questions which were rapidly muffled as politicians used the legend to exalt so-called 'Republican values'. Along with reservations about the veracity of her actions, no documentary evidence relating to her trial could be found. The story may simply have been fabricated because France, smarting from its ignominious defeat, needed a hero(ine).

Doubts notwithstanding, streets in La Réunion, a girls' school, and hotels were (and remain) named after her; on 19 July 1914, a statue was erected in her honour at Bièvres. A search on the Bibliothèque Nationale Française site, Gallica, gives over 1,000 'hits' for printed material and articles relating to her, many published in the late nineteenth and early twentieth century to provide uplifting material for children – and a reminder of the loss of Alsace-Lorraine. The controversy continues – while most historians are sceptical, others feel there are some elements of truth in the events. What is plain is that in the dark years between 1873 and 1914, France needed a heroic national figure, and Juliette Dodu could, at least with some stretching of the imagination, fulfil the role of France's new Joan of Arc.

Louise de Bettignies (1880–1918)

If questions remain unresolved about Juliette Dodu's espionage, none surround those of the woman dubbed the 'Jeanne d'Arc du Nord', Louise de Bettignies, a ruthless contemporary of Régina's, to whom fate has been much kinder. She is still considered one of France's greatest heroines. Whilst many thousands of words have been devoted to her story, parts of it would resonate with Aphra Behn, as at one point, vital information that Louise provided was discounted because … it came from a woman.

Louise's start in life was very different to Régina's. Born near Lille in Northern France, the seventh child of a formerly well-to-do Franco-Belgian aristocratic family, she nevertheless needed to earn her own living. Noted for her intelligence and linguistic abilities, she spoke French, German, Czech, Italian and English and could get by in Russian and Spanish, at the turn of the century she studied at Girton College, Cambridge. She worked as governess to several noble families although she declined the post of governess to the children of Archduke Franz-Ferdinand (of Sarajevo fame).

She returned to Lille just as the Great War erupted. On 12 October 1914, Lille fell into enemy hands and soon bristled with German soldiers – and a German spymistress. Eventually, Louise decided to join her family who had escaped to St Omer in non-Occupied France, a hazardous journey through Occupied Belgium, neutral Holland, onward to Folkestone and then back to Free France. The journey was even more dangerous as, sewn into the hem of her skirts, she was carrying over 300 tiny (forbidden) letters, written by people in Occupied France to those on 'the other side'. Postal communication between the two zones had been shut down. The first of countless actions to place her in considerable danger.

In Folkestone, where all immigrants were interviewed in the hopes of capturing enemy agents and infiltrators and recruiting potential spies, her linguistic capabilities impressed the Intelligence Services, always on the look-out for those with fluency in one or more of the combatant languages. Spymaster Captain (subsequently Major) Aylmer Cameron offered her employment working for the British in Occupied France. Initially claiming spying filled her with repugnance, partly driven, as Régina would be, by financial need, she finally accepted. As well as intensive training in map-reading and grid-referencing, she learned, as Régina and countless others were doing, to write in invisible ink on tissue paper which could be swallowed if needs be, on rice paper which does not make a noise when it is unfolded, to engrave minute letters on spectacle frames and place these over the lenses, and to conceal messages in shoe heels, umbrella handles, matchboxes as well as hems of skirts and hollowed out vegetables. Even stamps could conceal messages, either by writing on the envelope before affixing the stamp or meticulously cutting the perforations to conceal a message. These mundane items were the standard spy-kit of the era irrespective of whose side the spies were working for. Several envelopes held in Régina's files bear multiple stamps, some of whose edges have been tampered with. They may conceal messages now hidden to history.

Louise's remarkable brain and aptitude were soon apparent. Back in Lille in February 1915, she established escape routes for Allied soldiers and prisoners trapped behind the lines and provided information about German troop and train movements, zeppelin raids, munitions dumps and airfields. Having created a meticulous reduced map of the German lines with two thousand gun positions marked, this was cemented into the fittings of a courier's spectacles and the positions duly bombed.

Like Régina, she developed a spy network with multiple agents. One set reported on the movements of German troops around the Franco-Belgian border. Another division, comprising people who lived near Lille and who could justify frequent movement to the occupying authorities as well as seemingly 'invisible' women, provided a wealth of information about military hardware and troop numbers – similar information to that being relayed to Germany by Régina. At one point, Louise was behind the British bombing of a munitions depot at Tourcoing. The subsequent considerable loss of life did not, seemingly, weigh on her conscience.

In Folkestone, Spymaster Cameron could not 'speak too highly of the bravery, devotion and patriotism of this young lady. Her service to the British Intelligence is simply invaluable'. The German High Command began to call the 40km around which her networks operated the 'cursed' front because, out of nearly 700 miles of Front Line, this is where they seemed to suffer the greatest number of unexpected attacks, aerial bombardments and human casualties. The French High Command were less willing than the British to listen to her. One of her very last messages announced that the Germans were preparing a massive attack on Verdun in early 1916. The French commander who received the information dismissed it. How could a mere woman know this? The 162,308 French dead or missing of Verdun, not to mention the 100,000 German victims, may have wished he had been less dismissive of a woman's transmissions.

By the autumn of 1915, she knew that it was only a matter of time till her luck ran out. On 15 September, her right-hand agent, Marie-Léonie Vanhoutte, was apprehended and, unbeknownst to Louise, held in St Gilles prison in Brussels. Five weeks later, Louise was stopped by the Germans. Swallowing the message written on tissue paper which she needed to pass on via Holland, she too was thrown into St Gilles. Even her captors were impressed by her courage. During six months of questioning and probably torture, she never wavered. A fellow prisoner wrote, 'every means had been used in vain to make her speak'. Yet, 'she never showed signs of faltering, saying little and denying everything'.

The Germans planted a double agent in her cell. A common way of trying to break a spy as the plant appeared to lend a sympathetic ear; the French acted similarly when Régina was incarcerated. Eventually, enough incriminating evidence was gathered and in March 1916 the trial of Louise de Bettignies and Marie-Léonie Vanhoutte opened in Brussels. Only the penalty was in question; Louise's father traced his ancestry back to Charlemagne – would the Germans dare to execute as highborn a woman? Following a 'guilty' verdict, the death sentence was passed. It is hard to know whether it was the Spanish authorities' intervention with a plea for clemency, the notoriety and spectacular 'back-firing' of the Nurse Edith Cavell execution of October 1915, or her family's status that led to the death sentence being commuted to lifetime imprisonment with hard labour.

Treated as common, as opposed to political, prisoners, both women were sent to the notorious Siegburg prison, near Cologne in Germany; prison conditions were almost unbearable. Invoking the 1899 Hague Convention which forbids prisoners of war labouring in activities detrimental to their own side (Chapter 1, Article 6), Louise led revolts against prisoners being forced to work in German munitions factories. Thrown into solitary confinement in barbaric conditions in the freezing winter of 1917 she contracted pneumonia which turned to pleurisy. When she developed an abscess on the lung, minimal medical care was provided. She was operated upon in the prison in a room previously used for typhus patients.

Louise died on 27 September 1918, forty-five days before the Victory that she had done her utmost to hasten during her nine months' service as one of the Allies most successful spies. Responsible for the deaths of thousands of German soldiers and the loss of huge amounts of matériel, she probably never knew that on 20 April 1916, Maréchal Joffre had mentioned her in his dispatches.

In her invisibility lay her strength

From fifth century BC Sun Tzu, through to the 1899 Hague Convention and the musings of the Men of Letters, spies were written about in masculine terms. This cursory glance at a very few of the female spies of the modern era has demonstrated that despite five centuries separating the Marchioness of Northampton from Louise de Bettignies, their gender rendered them largely invisible and easily forgotten.

No male courtier would have had as intimate access to Queen Elizabeth I as that enjoyed by the Marchioness of Northampton. This allowed her to share intelligence with the queen's arch enemy, Philip II of Spain. Known from her girlhood as a copious letter-writer, Elizabeth of Bohemia, the Winter Queen's lengthy correspondence, which criss-crossed Europe, attracted little attention. Assumed simply to contain mere domestic 'gossip', she was working for her deposed husband's restoration to his briefly occupied throne. In the era of the now almost forgotten Anglo-Dutch wars, Aphra Behn could legitimately visit her late husband's native Holland and mingle with members of her own ex-patriot community, even when relations between England and Holland descended into all-out war.

During the American War of Independence, Anna Strong 'Mother-of-nine', as today's British tabloid press would describe her, would have been busy with her large family; washing on the line simply indicated that she was fulfilling her wifely and motherly duties, not sharing information with the Revolutionaries. In the American Civil War, Elizabeth Van Lew was demonstrating her caring feminine nature by taking small comforts to Northern soldiers imprisoned in Richmond, Virginia. No woman could possibly understand anything of military importance and so she could be allowed to visit 'Yankee' PoWs. Former slave Mary Bowser would have faded into the background in the 'Rebel' White House; few in the Confederate inner sanctum would have ever imagined that one of her colour and gender might be literate and gathering intelligence from the very heart of the Confederacy. On the other side of the Mason-Dixon Line, information contained in a 'beautiful roll of hair' may have affected the outcome of an early key battle in this bitter Civil War. In the brief Franco-Prussian war, Juliette Dodu was, initially at least, seen as continuing with her relatively lowly employment at the telegraphic office in Pithviers. Nevertheless, some believe that her actions and wire-tapping saved many French soldiers' lives. Moving forward to the Great War, it would be months before the German Commanders on the so-called 'cursed front' tracked down Louise de Bettignies. Tragically for both French and German soldiers, the French High Command, replicating Britain's errors regarding Aphra Behn's intelligence, dismissed Louise's evidence – once again because she was a woman.

Each of these women of widely varying social rank, educational background and ethnicity demonstrated that in the deeply patriarchal, even misogynistic society in which she lived and spied, her gender, which rendered her invisible in the public sphere, allowed her to strive for the cause which was dear to her heart. A cause that she was willing, and even at times was called upon, to pay for with her life. As with Régina, in these women's invisibility lay their strength.

Chapter 3

A Rebellious Teenager

Geneva 'la Riche', a far from Calvinistic City

Nowadays, most of us see Geneva as the rich and cosmopolitan city she has become. But at the turn of the twentieth century she was an outwardly sleepy, opulent merchant town comfortably nestled at the far end of the lake that (at least for English and German speakers) bears her name. With privileged access to the waterways of Western Europe, on the threshold of the Alps and the Northern Italian plains, Geneva was then, even more than today, an important geographical hub.

This was the city towards which one Joseph Avvico directed his thoughts in 1880. This young cobbler came from Pinerolo, a town and commune in Piedmont, northwestern Italy, fifty kilometers southwest of Turin on the river Chisone. By the end of the nineteenth century, Pinerolo had developed an excellent reputation for manufacturing and textile work. But poverty had recently increased and so Joseph embarked upon the roughly 300 kilometres trek over the Alps to make a new start. Geneva, with its total population of 101,595 including some 37,895 foreigners (of whom the majority were French), was his final stop after a nine-month journey.

If he had hoped to find riches, the young man was soon bitterly disillusioned. Near starvation led this proud Italian to frequent the 'soupe populaire' (soup kitchens) where, if you were amongst the lucky ones, you could grab a heel of dried bread and a cupful of cabbage soup. Like many Italian immigrants, he soon found himself in the 'underworld' manipulated by some of the city's richer, less scrupulous merchants. He scraped a living from small jobs and almost certainly supplemented his income by committing petty offences. Although no official records relating to him remain, the area of the city where he lived, les Eaux-Vives, leads one to conclude that he almost certainly served time in jail. Nowadays close to the city centre, in the 1880s Eaux-Vives was the 'dumping ground' where former inmates of the infamous Saint-Antoine Prison would squat. Both inmates and citizens nicknamed this Geneva prison 'la Discipline'. A moniker that was earned, if popular legend is to be believed, from the propensity of the wardens and the governor both to rule and to muster their men with a rod of iron. The harsh conditions were notorious and the municipal government boasted that this contributed to keeping the city neat and quiet, significant virtues in the eyes of citizens of the Calvinistic city of Geneva.

According to the immigration office, in 1881 Joseph temporarily left the city, which seems to have contributed to calming his rebellious spirit. He slipped across the border into neighbouring France as many, including his daughter, spies and deserters, would do some thirty years later. Working as a cobbler in nearby Saint-Julien-en-Genevois, he at last embarked upon his long awaited new life. Nothing specific is noted for the next couple of years.

The 'contrôle des habitants' (Cantonal Office of Population and Migration for the Canton of Geneva) records his reappearance in Geneva in late 1883, in the Petit-Saconnex area, now married to a laundress named Louise-Jeanne Crepet, native of Collonges, a small town in the adjacent French département of Ain. They had met in the nearby French town of Annemasse, an eventual stamping ground for spies making their way to and from Geneva. The couple settled at le Prieuré du Petit-Saconnex. The Palexpo (a large prestigious Convention Centre yards from the airport) now stands in an area that just over a century ago comprised working class tenements.

A year later, Joseph opened a small cobbler shop in the nearby Route de Ferney. His small business grew and gradually allowed him to live in modest comfort. On 27 July 1885, Louise gave birth to a daughter, christened Marie-Antoinette. With her mother continuing to work as a laundress and her father as a cobbler, the baby was often left in the care of neighbours, making her a loner at a very young age.

Little is known of either the early years of her childhood or young adolescence other than she attended the primary school for girls in Petit Saconnex. She briefly dances into view at the age of 15. As the new century dawned, a large crisis of field workers and rich landowners in neighbouring Ain threw dozens of young Frenchmen and women out of work and home. They were lured to 'Genève La Riche' as the city came to be nicknamed, seeing it as an Eldorado. For unexplained reasons, Marie-Antoinette participated in ransacking a local grocery shop near the outskirts of nearby Meyrin, then a small agricultural village (now a commuter town for the CERN laboratories). The teenager's record states she was involved in causing some damage to private property, as well as petty theft. No doubt anxious to maintain appearances with his clients, and worried his own somewhat troubled past may come back and haunt him, Joseph dispatched his daughter to her mother's family in Collonges. Troublesome Marie-Antoinette failed to settle down as her parents expected although she was apprenticed to a milliner, a very popular trade in the area and one that had fired the imagination of both novelists and many of the Impressionist French artists, including Dégas who explored the subject numerous times concentrating most of his attention on the beauty of the hats rather than the desperate poverty of many of their creators, poverty which pushed a number into prostitution. Perhaps unaware in Geneva of the enforced seediness of many milliners' lives, the Avvicos were undoubtedly relieved that their wayward daughter was following in her artisan father's footsteps. Almost certainly skilful, she nevertheless appears to have abandoned her training a year later. One is forced to wonder if something happened in Collonges that soured her attitude towards her mother's compatriots.

During the next three to four years Marie-Antoinette's lifestyle was one which in modern terminology would be called that of a rebellious teenager. She came and went from the parental home and fell in with a questionable local Geneva crowd; eventually she started being seen in the company of a young man whose business dealings included being a garage manager and tyre trader. He was to prove decisive in the years ahead and it is thanks to him and his nefarious ways that her life acquired its previously unimagined international slant.

The 'Devil's Bargain'

Turning the clock back approximately two decades to the 1880s, the time when Marie-Antoinette herself was growing up in Geneva, a small boy with the family name Cherix who would come to have a fateful impact upon her life and her political views, was being uprooted from this same city. His poorly-educated father had fallen in with a Frenchman whose immoral lifestyle, including gambling, had bankrupted and subsequently taken over the Cherix family business.

When he was 5 years of age this young boy, his siblings and their parents, moved just under 110 kilometers from Geneva to the town of Payerne in the adjacent canton of Vaud – to many Swiss, moving to a different canton resembles moving to another country rather than another county. Renowned for its Clunisian settlement and tenth century Abbey, Payerne is the capital of the Broye Vaudoise at the north-eastern border of the francophone canton. Proud of their town's heritage, which stretched as far back as the sixth century, the local citizens may have been unwelcoming to those who came from more cosmopolitan Geneva; the family never fully integrated with their new neighbours. His father finally drank himself to death and his mother never recovered from this loss, dying soon after. Hatred for the Frenchman who had brought his family to its knees, uprooted them and contributed to the death of his parents, was simmering inside the young Cherix who, with his three brothers, survived through lowly jobs and larger criminal offences.

To understand the young Cherix's trauma at being uprooted from Geneva to Payerne, and the part that this may have played in his loathing of the French, in his criminal career and, by one remove, in the recruitment and fate of Marie-Antoinette, it is worth pausing briefly over the idea of moving to another canton. For, although Switzerland is a 'country', it is helpful to think of it as twenty-six (twenty-five in 1914) small countries called 'cantons', some even 'half cantons', united by the mutual, nebulous, bond of the Pact of 1291 (which in reality only comprised the three founding cantons Uri, Schwyz and Unterwald). This led to the creation of the Helvetic Confederation (Switzerland) which other areas slowly joined. But all the subtlety lies in the fact that each canton was, and still is, sovereign in its legal and financial management as well as that of criminals. An offender could be considered a felon in one canton yet could move to another, even adjacent one, without their criminal record being transferred there or even known about. This was a weakness that the undoubtedly charming Cherix would exploit to the full in the coming years.

Aged 18 as the new century dawned and back in his native city, burning with hatred and a desire for revenge, the young Cherix who, unbeknownst to the Geneva cantonal authorities, had been convicted for theft and trafficking in the canton of Vaud, started weaving his web, one which would come to ensnare Marie-Antoinette. In the decade or so before the outbreak of war, he successfully acquired enough power to earn the reputation of being one of Geneva's most renowned mobsters. Yet he remained untouchable for he successfully kept himself at one remove from criminal activities. His underworld network contacts and businesses were as varied as they were surprising; they spread from cabarets, exotic dancers, alcohol, to smuggling food, cigarettes, toys, and clothes. But the jewel in his crown was tyres; rubber to be precise and rubber would have its part to play in Marie-Antoinette's life-story.

Rubber during the nineteenth and twentieth centuries was as valuable as copper is for electronics today. In an era newly conquered by automobiles, rubber was in the fast lane. Its price was soaring sky high, providing easy money for anyone who knew how to exploit the industrialised, as well as the military, world's insatiable appetite for this commodity essential to the dawning of the brave new world that was the twentieth century. Cherix was crafty and ruthless. Geneva, the border city, the hub between south-eastern and Western Europe became an overnight market place for goods from across the continent, including those supporting the motor industry. There was easy money to be made by those willing to function if not on the blind, then at least on the shady side of the law.

With his involvement in smuggling rubber, it is impossible to know whether Cherix became involved in what Adam Hochschild calls a war-time 'top-secret devil's bargain'; a chilling briefly-told tale, conducted, from neutral Switzerland's point of view, legitimately. By May 1915, the British Ministry of Munitions was struggling to provide officers and NCOs with high quality binoculars because pre-war, Germany was the optimum supplier of optical precision instruments. With the Battle of Loos being planned, the situation was at crisis point and even appeals to the British public to donate their own binoculars only yielded some two thousand pairs – King George V and Queen Mary donated four pairs each. Meanwhile, the British maritime blockade made it impossible for Germany to source the rubber essential to its war machine. So, working through an agent in neutral Switzerland, the belligerents struck their 'devil's bargain'. Germany would supply binoculars in return for rubber from Britain's colonies which would be routed (probably via Marseille where Marie-Antoinette was ensconced) through Switzerland to be collected at the German border.

My Name will be Régina Diana

A decade before this bargain was struck, rebellious Marie-Antoinette was already living her life on the shady side of the law using her innate resourcefulness to assist Cherix and smuggle tyres and mechanical parts across the Swiss border. A century ago, as is the case today, the cost of living and of goods was substantially lower in France than in Switzerland and, without the benefit of the twenty-first century's 'free movement of goods and people', many customers were willing to overlook the provenance of highly desirable commodities. Even before the war, not all customs officers were as assiduous in their duties as the authorities would have wished and, as would become very apparent during the war, some were easily corruptible. Although she could not have foretold this, voluptuous Marie-Antoinette's frequent pre-war forays across the border made her a familiar figure when she began crossing into and out of France for more nefarious reasons than the illicit acquisition of tyres and car parts, to further the business ambitions of Cherix who, back in his native Geneva, was, overtly at least, a '*garagiste*'.

Outwardly a respectable young businessman and generous donor to charity, Cherix was thriving as both a relatively small-time crook and manager of numerous cabarets and similar places of entertainment in the Quartier des Pâquis which stretched from Geneva's main station down to the lake, famed then as now for its luxury hotels including the Beau Rivage (noted by adored French music-hall singer Mistinguett as a prime location for recruiting spies). Many such establishments had been mushrooming since the urbanisation of the 1850s. Yet there was a dark underbelly to this fashionable area for, cheek by jowl with these hostelries, were the 'maisons closes' (brothels) and establishments euphemistically known as 'hotels de passe' where rooms could be rented by the hour, as well as the music halls, bistros and cabarets which were supplementing the income of Cherix and many other impresarios. Café-concerts and music halls flourished in Geneva in the closing years of the Belle Époque.

The Quartier des Pâquis, with its ideal location became Cherix's kingdom. Business was booming; young women of relatively dubious morality were drawn like magnets to the area. It was undoubtedly here where the still-rebellious Marie-Antoinette Avvico had first caught his eye. That she had given birth to a daughter in 1905, issue of what appears to have been a very short-lived marriage with one Louis Decosterd, does not seem to have bothered him. They rapidly became lovers and he set her up as his official mistress. Pale of complexion with the buxom figure associated with the 'belles femmes' of that period, at 6ft tall, she filled a room merely by her presence.

Thriving in this new opulent life Marie-Antoinette, now well acquainted, albeit relatively discreetly, with the night life of Geneva, had become a 'chanteuse lyrique' and performed in operettas in one or more of her lover's venues. Long before this would become her code-name, she chose her stage-name: Régina, Latin for 'queen', suited her attitude perfectly. Diana, the Greek goddess of hunting, gives a clear insight into her ambitions. Régina (as we will now call her) became a lynchpin in Cherix's 'empire'. So much so that contacts within the German intelligence with whom he had been entwined for some time and who were increasingly on the lookout for francophone Swiss with anti-French tendencies, began to take notice of her.

Intrigued by her, and eager to know more about this colourful singer, Cherix's German contacts summoned him to Zurich in early 1910; Régina Diana was to accompany him. Intelligence gathering was not a phenomenon born fully-fledged at the outbreak of hostilities. Far from being spawned by the war, the major powers had been busy refining their potential intelligence networks in anticipation of a major European conflict. Zurich, the largest city in Switzerland, conveniently located only twenty-four kilometres from the German border was, perhaps unbeknownst to the Swiss authorities, becoming a nest of spies with military and cultural attachés beginning to lay out their stalls for when war finally erupted. Cherix was by all accounts convincing and charming, as recruiters frequently were, as well as being ruthless and, significantly for the Germans who had spotted him, still ferociously opposed to France, sentiments which his lover shared.

Believing she was accompanying Cherix on a business trip, Régina was unaware that she was in fact being taken for a 'job interview' that would ultimately seal her fate. Perhaps unwittingly, she put on such a show that her lover's contact informed their chain of command that she could be a very suitable addition to the German stable should she be needed. She would have to be trialled and here her experience as a milliner would soon prove its worth. Frustratingly, she now disappears from the records for well over a year. However, without this trip to Zurich this flamboyant woman would have been nothing more than a petty smuggler, music-hall artiste and occasional prostitute.

Agent Régina Diana was set to become more deadly and more efficient than many of the spies whose names have been preserved in film, legend and history. Yet she has been side-lined to brief, repetitive clips in Australian and British newspapers and all but ignored (perhaps intentionally) by the press of both the country in which she was operating, and also the one where she had spent almost all of her formative years. Still overlooked today, a very brief article published in the 1 March 2015 *24 Heures* (Lausanne) contains several inaccuracies and significantly underestimates her contribution to a war fought not with guns, tanks and shells, but with invisible ink, postcards and meticulous observation. Neither physically attractive (by twenty-first century standards), nor gifted intellectually, she would nevertheless prove, as we are about to discover, resourceful enough to become one of Germany's most lethal non-firearm weapons.

Chapter 4

A Spy on the Loose

Si Vis Pacem Para Bellum (If you want peace, prepare for war)

If, in the decades leading up to war, spy novels were regularly on the 'Bestseller' lists, life mimicked art and shadowy figures were busy behind the scenes arranging the chess pieces necessary for fighting the intelligence war. Although some combatant nations were quicker out of the ante-bellum starting block than others, once Germany awoke to the need to invest millions of marks in the recruitment and training of spies, she was quick to deploy men and women across both neutral territory and lands they anticipated becoming 'the enemy'. Régina Diana was among this advance guard.

By January 1914, Régina, undeniably a small cog in a large wheel, was in Paris, working as a milliner in the east of the city, her workshop within sight of the great fortress of the Château de Vincennes, the French Military Headquarters where (often classified) information concerning the real power of both the French Army and Navy was held, data her employers desperately needed. Millinery was the perfect employment for a woman who wished to see without being seen. Those who frequented milliners' establishments would have barely glanced (other than lasciviously as certain French artists such as James Tissot demonstrate) at the assistants; they, like most owners of more affluent establishments, rarely saw hired help as individual human beings with at times their own hidden, subversive agendas.

Régina had positioned herself astutely. Her workshop headed by Madame Simone Lelavandier was the main provider of the French army officers' kepi. Arrogant young officers would flock to the shop desperate to show off. No doubt some boasted and blabbered about the importance of their work at the Château. Also, perhaps conscious that to the man in the field, those serving in staff offices were in 'cushy' jobs, they might have welcomed the sparkling eyes of a young milliner who would listen eagerly to the tales they had to tell.

Seemingly good at her trade, Régina became the workshop's 'première chapelière' and enjoyed the Parisian lifestyle which must have appeared glittering and sophisticated compared to that of Geneva. However, she regularly returned to Switzerland to see her mother, her lover, and her only child whose care Cherix was funding. These journeys between Paris and Geneva made her a familiar voyager to those who controlled the border – particularly useful when borders began to be closely watched.

Having established herself in Paris, the daytime milliner soon had a nocturnal second métier. One that few would have been surprised by as there is evidence in both art and literature that milliners were also (often forced by sheer necessity) 'good time girls'. Régina appeared to be more than willing to comfort officers and senior NCOs who were, to re-quote the contemporary euphemism, 'missing their wives', albeit according to the trial papers she was doing so relatively discreetly. Her lovers were less discreet and were quick to share information with her.

Partly stationed in Paris for nearly two years, both before and during the war, Régina managed to acquire considerable information pertaining to the French Army, its potential strength in terms of troop numbers, the composition of various arsenals along the Franco-German border and the preferred routes for re-fuelling the military encampments there. More importantly, she managed to gain intelligence on the tactics used by the French High Command. Nevertheless, there came a point, when Régina was becoming too visible. Her bosses were probably worried that she was starting to attract too much attention for she was one of the most popular 'accompagnatrices' of the Vincennes area. When the Germans decided, perhaps misguidedly from their point of view, to deploy her elsewhere, she was on the verge of acquiring information concerning the French Army's intended rail routes.

Pretexting the poor health of her now ageing mother, Régina left the Lelavandier workshop and returned to Switzerland for de-briefings which would have taken place in Zurich and the German Embassy in Bern; here she would undoubtedly have made the acquaintance of Germany's military attaché Otto von Bismarck. Having proved her worth in Paris, she would soon be deployed in the Southern and particularly Mediterranean areas of France where Germany would need accurate, regular information about Allied troop arrivals and departures, shipping and, should the war prove to be a long one, the equally important civilian morale. The Central Powers, all too aware that their limited access to the Mediterranean could be a severe handicap, wanted to minimise this geographic and strategic disadvantage. The German dilemma was where thus to send this woman who had already demonstrated her aptitudes. There were two contenders.

Toulon, once a sleepy little fishing port had, over the centuries, became not only the capital of the Var department but also one of France's most significant naval bases and of crucial importance during the era of fighting sail. Its fortunes ebbed and flowed during the Revolution but, since the age of Napoleon, its star had waxed brightly and, at the turn of the twentieth century, it had been granted the honour of harbouring France's high seas' fleet. (Parenthetically, it was in Toulon that a young naval lieutenant Jacques Cousteau, the 'father of underwater exploration' assigned to the Mediterranean fleet in the 1930s, began experimenting with swimming underwater using aviator's goggles.) The whole of the town and its outskirts would, during the war, be under intense scrutiny by military and civilian authorities alike, not to mention those who, like Régina, were seeking intelligence about France's Mediterranean fleet.

Sixty kilometres to the west of Toulon lies Marseille; the German High Command gambled that if war broke out, France's colonial troops and those of other allied forces would land not in Toulon but in Marseille as the area over which it spread was vaster than that available in Toulon, huddled at the foot of Mount Faron. Marseille's location enabled troops to be billeted in camps, trained, and 'processed' before being dispersed to the battlefields – and of course spied upon. It was thus correctly anticipated that Marseille, with its geographical advantages, would soon become a key entry point for the Western Theatre and that an exceptional agent would need to be deployed – one who could pass unnoticed because French counter-espionage would be all too aware of the port's importance.

In the late spring of 1914, Régina was once again on the move, briefly to Toulon then to Marseille. Her cover was the obvious one: 'chanteuse lyrique'. Café-concerts boomed in ante-bellum Marseille. She was ordered to befriend a high-ranking logistics officer whose position would give him access to virtually every piece of intelligence the Germans would require: information about troops, equipment, ammunition, arms, canon and transportation, both rail and naval. As well as being France's premier port, Marseille, was an important railhead linking the rest of France with the gateway to France's Empire as even a cursory glance at the so-called 'bible' of railway journeys, *Bradshaw's Railway Guide* of 1913, makes clear.

Germanic insight and organisation have long been admired and recognised and their early positioning of agents in anticipation of war is an excellent example of Teutonic forward planning. The high efficiency of agents such as Régina, who were already in the field, provided Germany and her allies with a clear advantage in August 1914, even if von Bismarck and other contributors to the two-volume *Espionnage Contre-Espionnage* translated from

German into French and published post-war, disingenuously implied that Germany was, pre-war, on the back foot.

Germany prized method and precision above all else. Habit and regularity came a close second. Régina displayed impressive levels of concentration and a rigorous approach to her missions. Irrespective for whose side they were working, spies acknowledged that if they were caught, they often, if not always, had only themselves 'to blame'; change was a high-risk factor. The more regular a person's movements, the more invisible they become and it is in this invisibility that the spy's strength so often lies. But for a run of bad luck, Régina, with her regular movements, may have remained forever in the shadows.

At the beginning of the war, Régina operated on two fronts: Paris and Marseille. Her usual routine appears to have been a fortnight in Paris, then a few days in Switzerland often staying with her mother, followed by a week in Marseille which, with the intensity of combat at this point centred upon the so-called distant Western Front, the shorter time spent in Marseille seemed adequate. The global nature of the conflict was not, initially at least, envisaged. Whether she reported back to her masters on a highly significant military scandal (discussed in Chapter 9) that had enveloped Marseille in late August 1914 we cannot be sure, but given the level of outrage and its effect upon civilians and their feelings towards the Union Sacrée, it almost certainly found its way to Zurich and thence to Berlin.

There are certain gaps in Régina's visibility at various points in 1915 and it is easy to argue that this is when she would have been undergoing additional training at either Antwerp or one of the other 'spy schools' established by the woman who became Germany's key spymaster, Elisabeth Schragmüller. Already an experienced operator, Régina would nevertheless have needed to enhance her skills in spy craft in time of war where the stakes are higher, the need for information greater, and ways of transmitting this need to be more refined. She certainly mastered the 'invisible ink' and miniature writing part of the course admirably. As the graphologist who analysed several of her postcards, and whose evidence played a key role in the prosecution's case, makes clear, copious information was concealed behind the simple 'Bons baisers Marcelle' (Love and kisses Marcelle) greetings she sent to one A. Duchilio at the Pension Simplon in Zurich, one of the frequent occasions when she used the hotel letter-drop ploy used by many spies. She would also have been drilled in military and naval reconnaissance, essential in a port town, as well as learning how to vet potential agents and extend her own ring. Like the Frenchwoman Louise de Bettignies, she was both an acute observer and also commanded her own network.

The wayward Marie-Antoinette of the 1900s, who seemed to lack staying power, had now developed total drive, commitment, and control of her mission. By 1916, with the network she commanded seemingly numbering up to twenty people placed in key locations including Marseille's vital docks, co-ordination, discipline and precision were vital. Ships brought troops into Marseille for transit to the Western Front from Britain's Dominions as well as from Russia, and they left with men and hospital personnel destined for Salonika. Information she and her ring supplied about these troop and ship movements was of vital interest to those for whom she was working. Régina's ring acted on three distinctive fronts and many of her agents were never uncovered. Her web would eventually spread from Paris to Marseille, from Crest to Zurich and from Geneva to Algiers with Pinerolo (in the Northwestern region of Piedmont, Italy) and Berlin as occasional hubs. Thousands of miles stretched across five countries and two continents … enough to make [the ineffective] Mata Hari blush.

'Ton gosse qui t'aime' (Your little kid who loves you)

As Marseille's strategic importance increased, it became Régina's key base as early as March 1915 – the time when men were sailing for Gallipoli via Marseille. Although she returned to Paris for brief periods to gain information from Vincennes, her main mission had become the relaying of information concerning the troop movements in and out of this crucial port. She had ingeniously forged a contact with a captain attached to the logistic corps of the colonial troops' high command with the express aim of acquiring intelligence relating to the incoming flow of soldiers from France's African and North African possessions for France, like Great Britain, turned to her colonies for additional manpower.

Based in Algiers, a naïve officer had 'fallen' for Régina, whom he had met in a tavern on Marseilles' waterfront. Whether this was one of the many 'maisons closes' (brothels) in the area we will never know. One of the countless lonely men frequenting the watering holes in Marseille, he was ripe for her plucking. On leave for a couple of weeks, they quickly began a relationship and she was never to release her grip on him. Little did he know that he was the pawn that she had been seeking. The countless postcards (some are preserved in her files) they exchanged would undoubtedly have seemed to any censor who might have glanced at them to be between one of the many Frenchwomen who had adopted the role of marraine de guerre, or 'godmother' to lonely French soldiers who were eagerly writing and receiving cards from so-called 'godsons'. This relationship, which would have a significant impact upon many women other than Régina and indeed the morale of countless poilus, is explored in Chapter 9. In many of these letters and postcards, just as in the ones between Régina and her 'catch', proclamations of affection became ever more pronounced.

This gullible, undoubtedly lonely, officer's letters and postcards provided her with regular updates of his work as a logistics coordinator. On at least three occasions, he offered to take Régina on a tour of the Algiers barracks and arsenals – a key area for France's military effort; all French colonial soldiers, be they from Algeria, Morocco, Tunisia for the Maghreb [North Africa] troops or from Senegal, Mali and the Ivory Coast, would assemble and undergo training in Algiers before being embarked for deployment across various fronts.

To fully understand Algiers' strategic importance, all that is needed is a quick glance at a map. Like its British counterpart Gibraltar, the home base for Britain's Atlantic Fleet and used as a forming-up point for Allied convoys, the Algerian capital Algiers, with its position in the occidental part of the Mediterranean, was an ideal jumping-off point not only for troops being sent to the Western Front but also ones being prepared for the Middle Eastern Front. It benefitted from being only 754km (by sea) from metropolitan France, but remote enough to be safe from an enemy attack.

Once formed into trained and equipped battalions, many troops from France's colonies crossed the water to fight in the bloody trenches of northern France. Crucially, Régina's new lover and his staff in Algiers were responsible for forming these battalions, arranging for their deployment to the front where they were most needed, and were responsible for the intricacies of their transportation to the required theatre, including the Somme. They were master puppeteers in the highly complex world of military logistics; he and his unit were of crucial importance with regard to incoming reinforcements for France and her allies. Régina, and no doubt her handlers in Germany, considered him 'the goose that laid the golden egg'.

They stayed in touch throughout 1916. He was generally sent to Marseille every two months and they stayed at the 'Grand Hotel des Princes' Place de la Bourse, once used by Napoleon as his headquarters for a few nights in 1796, situated relatively close to the busy port of Marseille. That she could afford such luxurious accommodation (and even received post here) indicates the depths of Germany's purse when valuable information was at stake. One of spymaster Elisabeth Schragmüller's hallmarks was her willingness to pay generously and provide agents with a substantial expense account where necessary. Deeply ironically in view of Régina's role as a siren or mermaid whose singing in Greek mythology lured men to their watery graves, two mermaids supporting a balcony are a central feature of the hotel – the only such statues in Marseille.

For those who even noticed them, the couple were often together in restaurants and waterfront cafés, once again demonstrating how a visible, regular routine can lead to invisibility. Who would think twice about a young officer in the company of an attractive young artiste from one of the nearby café-concerts, performing her supposedly patriotic duty by entertaining a brave soldier; such couples were ubiquitous in Marseille, perhaps he was just prolonging his evening's entertainment. By 1916, women were actively encouraged to raise the morale of troops on leave who were far from home and family; the songs sung every night in the café-concerts and which were belted out so lustily by the audience and the artistes were a timely reminder of this patriotic duty. As he would subsequently confess, he was blinded by his love for her, she made things so easy and her seemingly carefree character and witty conversation made her so lovable. Yet this lovable woman to whom he was soon referring as 'Mon amour' and signing off, 'ton gosse qui t'aime' (Your kid who loves you), was a redoubtable, cunning and ruthless siren who had lured him into her schemes.

As well as gathering and forwarding information concerning naval activity and incoming troops so innocently and helpfully provided by her lover, Capitaine Lefebvre, Régina's 'patch' still included Paris where she had conveniently become well acquainted with the inner circle of a high-ranking officer serving within the Place de Guerre, the headquarters of the French Army. Although the name of this gentleman is not in the public domain, it is highly probable he may even have been the general of a brigade. Exercising what appear to have been her considerable charms, there is every indication that she was adept at turning their 'pillow talk' towards movements of troops destined for the Western Front. But it was not only pillow talk in which she was engaged. Considerably raising the stakes and the risks she was taking, she would extricate and then commit to memory documents from his briefcase. This latter ploy is again indicative of an agent trained by the ruthless Elisabeth Schragmüller. She held those with powerful memories in great respect and memory skills interested her more than an agent's academic education or moral code.

The captain in Marseille and the officer in Paris were far from Régina's only contacts. We will never know the full list of her informers but the inquiry following her arrest attests to at least another five, including three holding crucial roles for those with ulterior motives: a dock worker, a merchant sailor, and a post office clerk. The first two would have provided her with crucial inside information about shipping; of course knowledge about merchant shipping is almost as valuable as that about troop numbers when trying to piece together strategic information. As all combatant nations discovered, a starving population becomes ever less patriotic. The postal clerk could report on information written on the ubiquitous postcards that connected families in wartime. If postcards from the Front were censored, exchanges between civilians were not subject to the same level of scrutiny. Once again, we can detect Schragmüller's hand, as she was deeply interested in civilian morale; while the postal clerk could not open letters, postcards contain insights which help create the bigger picture. Hidden within one of the captured and decoded postcards, she mentions the depths to which civilian morale in Marseille was plummeting. Information about army morale also appears on several of her lover's cards; he longs for this 'accursed war' to be over.

Régina's familial situation enabled her to deflect suspicion from her regular absences from her two main centres of operation. Her Swiss residency gave her a legitimate reason to be away for shorter or longer periods of time. In Paris, she generally claimed that she had a sick mother to care for. In Marseille, a relative in a sanatorium in the Swiss Alps joined the sick mother as cast-iron excuses. This so-called 'Aunt Louisa' was, as she revealed during interrogation, the alias of an individual named Louis with whom her mother was in close contact, he would hand over the fee, 1,700 French francs, for the information received. To watchful eyes in Geneva, sojourns in Marseille were easily explained. The warm climate and the sea air suited her vocal chords and, perhaps to deflect attention should the letters be opened, mother and daughter discuss their own and Régina's aunt's health in their correspondence. Few of those who were familiar with café-concerts' and music halls' smoky atmospheres and poor air quality would have seen sea air cures as anything other than a sensible precaution taken by a woman whose livelihood depended upon her powerful lungs.

A further asset was her daughter now being educated at Cherix's expense in Crest; who would think twice about a mother sending cards to a child at a boarding school or corresponding with those responsible for her care? Classified information was often relayed from Paris to Switzerland via Crest, which the caring mother would subsequently visit, staying at the Hotel de France where the owner, a Mme Barruyer, commented in a letter to Régina, that she always brought some 'gaieté' with her and cheered them up. Crest's geographical location far from the Front meant that little attention would be directed towards epistolary exchanges between women in this area. Once in Crest, Régina would retrieve the card and forward it to Switzerland, sometimes for the attention of Mlle Marie-Louise Févarotto, c/o Pension Walter in Zurich.

Marie-Louise Févarotto, as the court papers reveal, was also acting under an alias; her married name was Noverraz although she had divorced her husband. Possibly of Swiss-German origin (her maiden name was Muller) but born in francophone Switzerland and living in Lausanne, she was a near contemporary of Régina's and was part of her ring; their sojourns in Paris and Marseille sometimes overlapped. In Zurich, which Févarotto frequently visited, the authorities considered her contacts 'doubtful' (douteux), she was in 'intimate' relationships with both an Italian and a Greek citizen. Having been detained at Bellegarde near the Geneva border (also a frequent crossing point for Régina), she had slipped through the French authorities' net, she had been released and they never again closed in on her. In terms of intelligence gathered in Marseille, Régina's and Févarotto's Italian connections proved useful. Information sent to Pinerolo was, with the assistance of one of the Avvico cousins, transmitted to Régina's mother in Geneva. With Marseille's numerous Italian immigrants no one would have thought twice about postcards sent to Italy. Yet the cards' final destination was Zurich, occasionally the Hotel Simplon, but more frequently Pension Walter.

The Pension Walter was considered the Ritz for Spies. As surely as the Ritz Hotel is a major landmark for the rich and powerful, so was the Pension Walter for those whose life was spent in the shadows. Régina's file makes it apparent that by 7 February 1917, the French authorities were aware of the Pension's hidden purpose but, thanks to this German-speaking area of Switzerland's lack of true neutrality, Zurich authorities chose to turn a blind eye and there was little concrete that France could do other than raise concerns with the Swiss authorities. As one French Swiss postcard dating from March 1916 (see the plate section of this book) demonstrates, by this stage in the war 'Mademoiselle Neutralité' was, in the eyes of many, truly dead.

Just another postcard

In this now war-weary world, revolution and political unrest were brewing. France was bending under the burdens placed upon all citizens by the war effort; burdens which, as they had done for the previous two and a half years, invariably weighed most heavily upon the poor. To add to the widespread hardship, the previous two winters had been the harshest in recorded history. Discontent was growing steadily and reached a peak in what became known as the 'sugar and coal crises'. Despite facing their own considerable civilian unrest, the German authorities were eager to gather maximum information about disturbances taking place across France. Régina was now charged with supplying intelligence on civilian and military matters. Once again, she complied.

Morale was close to breaking point while prices continued to rocket, some, as Marseille historian Jean-Yves Le Naour points out, by as much as 180 per cent between 1916 and 1917 alone. The distress this caused, particularly among the families of poilus, whose allowances had not increased and who were now living below the bread line, cannot be overestimated. With an army interminably dug-in along the Western Front, with soldiers' morale plummeting ever lower, this was an inapposite time to be facing civilian unrest. Riots spread across many parts of France, which the government quelled sometimes by sending in armed police forces.

Temporary salvation was achieved in December 1916. The small city of Verdun, the final resting-pace of nearly a quarter of a million men, had become the site of one of the bloodiest battles of the war. Now, after months of suffering, the engagement had at last reached its conclusion. While it was hard for those countless thousands of families whose loved ones had died or been mutilated at Verdun to see it in this light, the French authorities, according to Charles Sorrie, 'orchestrated' this as a Victory which the nation could celebrate. But a second more decisive victory was badly needed. A new offensive was planned – yet it turned into a disaster. Some responsibility can be laid at the door of Agent Régina Diana, or, more precisely, thirty-seven of her post cards. The thirtieth was the one that set the cat among the pigeons.

Spies need to see but not be seen; the moment they appear in the full light of day, their lives are in mortal danger. Régina was about to appear on the French authorities' radar and, with the spotlight shining firmly upon her, she would be unable to creep back into the shadows. Probably all agents would agree that over confidence is the spy's worst enemy. To slacken one's guard and consider the opponent as less cunning is the cardinal mistake. When all is apparently running like clockwork, only the foolhardy drop their guard. A combination of inattentiveness and a heating stove brought Régina's house of cards tumbling down. For, as happened with several of the spies mentioned throughout this book and countless others, Lady Luck also entered the lists.

Whatever information an agent has succeeded in gathering is useless until it is delivered to handlers and those whom, in modern terminology, we might call the backroom staff. The intelligence war, like the hot one, is fought with the technology of the era. The great dilemma is how to pass highly classified information without arousing suspicion. Equally important is how to avoid the spy getting caught should their dispatches fall into the wrong hands. While intensive training in these crucial aspects of spy craft were provided at all spy schools, each agent in the field had to select and refine the tricks that had been taught – and never to become complacent.

Irrespective of the technology or techniques used, a spy's objective is to ensure the information for which they have placed their life in jeopardy reaches those whom it is intended to serve using the most expeditious means available. While twenty-first century spooks may use electronic equipment, social media and the ubiquitous mobile telephones, in the era of the First World War, postcards were in their heyday. There were postcards for everything and anything: flowers, food, landscapes, girls, and poilus. Almost every accoutrement of modern and wartime life was depicted. It is impossible to overestimate the part they played in this deadly war fought in the shadows. These small pieces of card paper were robust enough to be manipulated by post office personnel and reach their destination in a decent condition – the sheer quantity of wartime postcards still available to purchase is testimony to their sturdiness. Their visibility and thus, ironically, their invisibility, was their greatest asset. As messages were not even enclosed in an envelope, they were far less likely to arouse the suspicion of censors who, even in neutral Switzerland, now had the power to open letters and read the contents. No one in their right mind would send classified information on a post card … or would they?

Irrespective of postcards' ubiquitousness and the numbers exchanged during the war, the messages of those using them for nefarious reasons had to appear anodyne. From the sending of the cards to their arrival at their ultimate destination on the handler's desk, an average of five people would handle and potentially read the card, so the true message had to be rendered invisible. Stretching back into pre-History and Ancient Egypt, steganography, and in particular concealing of messages by using invisible ink, remained a preferred method of communicating covert information. As spies and agents working centuries before Régina had discovered, invisible ink is easy to both manufacture and use. The agent simply writes the intended coded message in invisible ink which often had a lemon juice base. Once the ink was completely dry, he or she would then proceed to write an innocuous text on the post card using, in the days before ballpoint and felt-tip pens, fountain pen. Yet as *Abteilung IIIb*'s head of staff noticed, regular ink written over the invisible ink changes colour through oxidisation, thereby becoming a tell-tale indication that there is a second, hidden inscription on the paper. The solution to that major setback was to write the decoy message in … squid or octopus ink.

This organic ink, unlike commercial ink, did not react to the acidity developed by invisible inks with a lemon juice base. One major further advantage of squid ink was that it could be quickly erased by simply applying a damp cloth over its surface. Once the displayed message was wiped off the usefully thicker than writing paper postcard, one final step remained: gently heat the card and its secrets are revealed. The ingenuity of this method is that apart from squid ink, which was not available everywhere, no special equipment was required other than the ability to heat the card.

> ***'The night mail crossing the border'***
> *This is the night mail crossing the border…*
> *Letters for the rich, letters for the poor,*
> *The shop at the corner, the girl next door…*
> *Gossip, gossip from all the nations…*
>
> *(From 'The Night Mail' by W. H. Auden)*

In very early February 1917, one of Régina's postcards was covering the 417 kilometres from Marseille to Geneva on the night mail train. The post wagon was heated by a large wood-burning stove. A postal employee was sorting the post in readiness for the train's arrival in Lyon. Letters and postcards were scattered across the main sorting table close to the stove. The hour was advanced and the radiating heat had raised the temperature to near tropical. So much so that something strange began to happen to one card. To the worker's bemusement, phoenix-like, a second message began to appear. This seemingly innocent-looking postcard was not what it seemed to be. But, as Shakespeare's Hamlet noted, 'when sorrows come, they come not single spies but in battalions'. A battalion of sorrows would soon await pro-German Agent Régina Diana.

Once the train arrived in Lyon, the observant employee handed the card to the local police station; it was rushed to Paris and the military police for further analysis. What they discovered horrified them. The results of their scrutiny were disseminated both nationwide and along the border running from Basel to Geneva. The Swiss authorities, desperate to protect the

Confederation's neutrality which was ever more fragile in the eyes of both France and Germany, were, outwardly at least, determined to clamp down on potential networks trying to communicate on either side of their porous borders. That France now appeared to have gathered hard evidence that a large German spy ring was demonstrably working out of Switzerland dealt a blow to Swiss counter-espionage pride. Vexed and eager to expunge any perceived (and no doubt genuine) previous failings, they worked tirelessly to uncover what was going on.

They did not have to wait long; in a one-week period, four postcards sent to Switzerland were traced back to Marseille. Not a difficult undertaking as the cards were all sent from the same post-box situated at the intersection of the Canebière and Place des Templiers. Now known as 'the road to nowhere' and the stamping ground of society's outcasts, in the 1910s Canebière was the hub of café and chic life in Marseille. One must assume that Régina had become slightly careless because spies were, for obvious reasons, generally encouraged to vary not only those to whom the cards were addressed, but also the post box from which they were sent. On 5 March 1917, Régina was arrested as she was preparing to dispatch her thirty-eighth [known to the authorities] postcard. While the first step which led to her downfall was a stroke of bad luck, the subsequent ones can be laid at her door, namely sending so many cards in such a short time span and the over use of the same post box. Or, was she only using this box? Were cards being posted elsewhere either by her or accomplices and reaching their intended recipients? We will never know.

Régina may have thought that she had mastered the art of both disguising her handwriting and concealing what she had written. However, as the court papers pertaining to the case reveal, the authorities sent this 'night train' post card and three subsequent ones which they had intercepted to a graphologist who was retained as an expert witness by the La Seine Tribunal in Paris. In a damning and copious report, (fortunately typed as his own handwriting is near illegible!) this Mr Hugues took readers through the amassed evidence quite literally letter by letter. He explained why there was no doubt that the cards addressed to Zurich that he had scrutinised, outwardly signed by one 'Marcelle' were, like the hidden messages they contained, from the hand of none other than Régina Diana. To allay any possible doubts, he used red ink to show the way a letter was formed in invisible ink and, using blue ink, how this corresponded to her 'normal' writing. Proud of his work and his esoteric area of expertise, he signed his document with many flourishes. Perhaps fittingly, his evidence comprises the final ten of the 480 pages which document the case against her and the proceedings of the trial. It was the final nail in her coffin because the information the cards contained was dynamite.

Régina was relaying intelligence to Zurich and subsequently to Berlin pertaining to civilian unrest, the army and the navy (not only the French ones). She reported that as well as the mustering of over 4,000 British and Canadians troops who were departing for north-eastern France, leave (*permissions*) was becoming ever rarer – usually an indication that a 'big push' was imminent. Aware of the importance of her intelligence, she duplicated (possibly triplicated or even quadruplicated) it; of the confiscated cards, one card was, as was frequently the case, addressed to Févarotto at Pension Walter, the other to 'A. Duchilio', Pension Simplon. It is tempting to surmise that these two accomplices were not the only recipients of this and indeed much of her other information. Court papers reveal that she corresponded with a Mme Joussot in Paris, with Mme Barruyer in Crest as well as with her mother in Geneva. Schragmüller taught her spies to use multiple 'drops' when it was crucial that data was passed quickly and accurately.

The confiscated cards did not only relay intelligence about civilian unrest and troop numbers congregating in Marseille. They also contained information about men arriving on two transport ships from an area that we now associate more readily with calamitous natural disasters than with the First World War. Troops were arriving from Haiti, they were due to be equipped and then, 'in about ten days', would be embarking for Salonika. Once decrypted, what these two cards revealed would be enough for the entire weight of France's counter-espionage forces to be unleashed, for they provided the authorities with the firm evidence needed to enable them to move legitimately from surveillance to detention.

Still today, reading about the number of troops massing in Marseille awaiting to be sent north sends a shiver down the spine. They were destined for a ridge in northern France where the authorities were planning what would turn into an engagement with calamitous consequences. Some of them would be amongst the 271,000 French casualties sustained at the Chemin des Dames.

Considering this battle, Wikipedia states that French General Robert 'Nivelle had underestimated the enemy's defensive preparations; the Germans had created a network of deep shelters in old underground stone quarries below the ridge where their troops took shelter from the French barrage'. The German commanders' defensive works may well have been extended thanks to intelligence received from one of their country's best agents. One of Régina's confiscated cards had alerted her handlers to preparations being made for a major offensive in this area towards the end of March – others may well have reached their destination before the authorities closed in on her. Turning to the battle itself, the horrific loss of life in the first and all subsequent days, the slow evacuation of the wounded, and the lack of logistical preparations, all contributed not only to the resignation of Nivelle but also to the French mutinies and the ensuing executions of 1917.

The intelligence supplied by Régina in March 1917 relating to the forthcoming French Chemin des Dames offensive represents her at the peak of her powers. Her informant network extended from Paris to Algiers to Marseille back to Geneva and onwards to Zurich. Her informants ranged across the military and social spectra and gave her access to information covering strategic troop movements as well as what was happening on the dockside. Yet her modus operandi, successful for over two and a half years, was ending. Her arrest was imminent. However, in order to fully understand her story, we should immerse ourselves at this stage in the world that had been Régina's: neutral Switzerland and the nest of spies that had spawned her, the importance of song in wartime France, as well as the somewhat seedy, war-traumatised world of Marseille with its booming café-concert and music hall culture which had allowed her to flourish and develop her network.

Chapter 5

Kilometre Zero: The Struggle for Neutrality

Nineteenth century Switzerland had an enviable reputation as a peaceful country, welcoming refugees, highborn immigrants, migrant workers, tuberculosis patients and those with leisure time to enjoy and money to spend. Its renowned hotels, sanatoria, magnificent scenery and crisp mountain air were widely extolled. This was the Switzerland in which Régina Diana grew up and, like others of her class and background, even before hostilities broke out, she would prove ripe for picking by the powerful recruiters and spy masters who, some with well-established ante-bellum bureaus, fanned out across the Swiss Confederation enticing spies to their cause. During the dark years of 1914–1918, the divisions between the Swiss themselves, the far from neutral leanings of the highest echelons of the military, and the seemingly never-ending spy scandals, tainted the once pure air and rocked the country to its very core.

To fully understand this world which was Régina's, we need to consider Switzerland from a vantage point little known today, even by many Swiss themselves. During the First World War Switzerland was a nation that was from the very outset, and would remain, deeply divided, although most 'ordinary' citizens strove to cling to the concept of Swiss Neutrality.

Neutral Switzerland on the eve of war

By the end of the period that historians often called the 'long' nineteenth century [up to August 1914], the concept of neutrality had become increasingly formalised; a set of international statutes ensured that neutral states would act in pre-determined ways should war break out. Although by 1914 several European states had declared their intention of remaining neutral in time of conflict, the one that had the greatest impact upon Régina Diana and other spies' stories, was Switzerland which some historians argue had become neutral almost by accident.

For Olivier Meuwly, neutral Switzerland as we know it to-day only dates back to the 1815 Congress of Vienna when Austria, France, Great Britain, Prussia and Russia (the main belligerents who would take to the stage again

100 years later) imposed 'perpetual neutrality' on the then nineteen, cantons of the Swiss Confederation. Meuwly considers 'there was no project for neutrality; circumstances dictated that Switzerland would be forced into neutrality by others'.

Forced into neutrality or not, the 1870–1871 Franco-Prussian war confirmed in the Swiss collective conscience the advantages of this political path. Bystanders to a war being waged close to their borders which culminated in a humiliating French defeat and formation of the German Reich, according to Carlo Moos, French-speaking Western Switzerland saw these events as a disaster, and German-speaking Eastern Switzerland as a triumph; fortuitously, their country's neutral status had ensured they remain outside the fray.

At the dawn of the First World War, Switzerland was trilingual. Out of a population of 3,828,431, about seventy-three per cent was German speaking, with many Swiss Germans having close cultural, educational and extended family links with Germany – the University of Heidelberg was even referred to as the 'first Swiss University' thanks to the number of Swiss students. About twenty-two per cent of the Swiss population were francophone – the cantons of Vaud, Geneva and Neuchatel were exclusively French speaking; Valais and Fribourg were bi-lingual. Pierre Du Bois argues that the cultural and military ties between the French-speaking Swiss (Swiss romands) and France were far more tenuous than those of the German-speaking Swiss with Germany; communality of the French language had not translated into what he terms 'cultural osmosis'. He even concludes that not insignificant numbers of French-speaking Swiss communities, particularly the 'haute bourgeoisie' of Geneva, the 'noblesse neuchateloise', as well as the conservative Catholics of Fribourg, were traditionally sympathetic to Prussia. The remaining five per cent of the population lived in the one Italian-speaking canton, Tessin. Swiss historians state that culturally the Tessinois felt closer to the French as opposed to German speakers and their natural instincts even before Italy entered the war in May 1915, veered against the Central Powers.

Switzerland had experienced an explosion of immigration the previous decades – their presence would impact significantly upon wartime Switzerland. According to Robin Cohen, by 1914, an estimated 600,000 foreigners (15.4 per cent of the population) lived in Switzerland. The 12 January 1917 *Journal de Genève* informed readers that in 1910, 219,000 German, 202,000 Italian, 63,000 French and 41,000 Austrian were resident in Switzerland, forming the majority, but not the entirety, of the émigré population; the *Journal* adds that forty-two per cent of Geneva's population (71,844) was foreign. Du Bois reveals that 60,000 Germans lived in the canton of Zurich, 40,000 in Basel, 25,000 in Saint Gallen and 12,000 in Bern. Of the foreigners living in Geneva, 35,000 were French and 5,500 German with another 7,700 Germans in the adjacent canton of Vaud. Even before the war, the liberal bourgeoisie and French-speaking Swiss had expressed fears about the numbers of German residents who they felt were dominating the immigrant community and 'Prussianizing' Swiss culture, particularly as there were Germans in all professions including the Press and university posts. There were, surprisingly, more native German than French professors at the francophone universities of Geneva, Lausanne and Neuchatel. A German citizen was even head of the Bern Tourist Office. Naturalised in November 1914, he was subsequently, accused of spying for Germany. Would, many Swiss wondered, the majority of these foreigners respect their host country's neutrality in time of war?

The other key player in Western Europe's neutrality field was Belgium. By mid-July 1914, with a European war increasingly likely, the Belgian government underlined its intention of abiding by the country's neutral status. As those with only a very passing knowledge of the opening days of the First World War know, the violation of Belgium's neutrality played a key role in setting the continent ablaze.

Keeping a close and anxious eye on the battle of wills developing between Germany and Belgium, and the high probability of a German invasion of Belgium, on 1 August 1914 (the Swiss National Day), the Swiss Federal Council ordered the Swiss Army to mobilise, not to go to war but to protect the nation's borders. This, they assured a now jittery population, was simply a precautionary measure designed to send a message to the 'Great Powers' that Switzerland would, should need arise, adopt all necessary measures to defend her neutrality, a message already conveyed to European governments on 31 July 1914, reiterated on 3 August, and formally proclaimed on 4 August. Far from this contravening the Confederation's neutral status, the 1907 Hague Convention had made plain that 'The fact of a neutral power repelling, even by force, attacks on its neutrality cannot be considered as a hostile act.' Switzerland – or indeed any other state's rights to mobilise their army in time of war, had been enshrined in law. But they had also to ensure that their country acted in a scrupulously neutral fashion – significantly, this included preventing spies being recruited in, sent out from, or in any way using, the Confederation's territory for their nefarious activities. Switzerland had to be seen as favouring no belligerent nation.

Although the Swiss Government reassured citizens that they believed French and German assurances that Swiss neutrality would be respected, nothing would be left to chance. The most pressing concern was to appoint a wartime Head of the Army or 'General of Switzerland'. Unsurprisingly, due to the linguistic imbalance of the population, most high-ranking officers hailed from the German-speaking cantons, many had received military training in Germany. After intense, acrimonious lobbying, Colonel Ulrich Wille, was not unanimously appointed on 3 August 1914. Three German speaking cantons joined all francophone ones in opposing this selection, favouring instead Theophile Sprecher von Brunegg.

It is unsurprising that the appointment was somewhat contentious: Wille had, like many Staff officers in the Swiss Army, undergone military training in Germany where he had spent a number of years; he had a reputation for supporting Prussian militarism, and in 1912, with considerable fanfare and jubilation, he had directed the Swiss Army manoeuvres which Kaiser Wilhelm II had attended during his official visit to Switzerland. Hinting at things to come, these manoeuvres had proved controversial, referred to disdainfully by some sections of the (predominantly francophone) Swiss press as the 'Kaiser's manoeuvres'; other journalists excitedly recounted the events, positive feelings for the Kaiser extending to his Reich. (In the novel *La Suisse dans un miroir,* one character even suggests that Wille's election was almost imposed upon Switzerland by the Kaiser in return for a guarantee of neutrality.) To cap it all, Wille was married to Countess Clara von Bismarck, the former German Chancellor's daughter. Francophone Lieutenant-Colonel Arthur Fonjallaz even suggested Wille was elected because the Swiss Federal Council (which only had one francophone member), like most of the Swiss GCHQ (État-Major) anticipated a rapid German victory and were keen to be seen to be aligned with the victors. Historian Christophe Vuilleumier notes that only five Swiss officers with the rank of major or above were known to show anti-German leanings.

Some contemporary Swiss journalists saw Wille's appointment as a pragmatic choice. Well-respected by the German High Command for his military acumen, his position as General of Switzerland would discourage Germany from taking a short-cut through Switzerland to invade France, thereby compromising Swiss neutrality; nevertheless, as a precautionary measure, troops were rushed to areas seen as potential flash points.

Reporting on the proceedings which led to Wille's appointment on 3 August, the *Gazette de Lausanne* (the most widely read French language newspaper in Switzerland) reminded readers of the need to support the new general who, immediately after his elevation, had sworn an oath to defend Swiss neutrality. Perhaps attempting to rally French-speaking citizens behind the new commander, the report went so far as to state that the Wille family were originally from French-speaking Switzerland. Nevertheless, whilst the press report painted Wille in a sympathetic light, an editorial hinted that much jockeying for power and position had occurred behind the scenes until the Federal Council – a seven-person executive had, to quote the newspaper, 'forced the hand' of the Federal Assembly.

Demonstrating that Swiss newspapers did not speak in a unified voice even if they wrote in the same language, one very widely read Geneva newspaper, the *Journal de Genève,* simply reported Wille's appointment and gave little information about the dispute surrounding this. A Swiss journalist, Louis Dumur, who had long left his native Geneva to write for the French newspaper *Mercure de France,* would in time accuse the *Journal* (in whose pages Régina would come to figure briefly) of being pro-German. In Dumur's eyes, the appointment of Wille demonstrated that irrespective of many 'ordinary' Swiss citizens' undoubted neutrality, the Swiss political élite had shown its hand – they were, emotionally at least, on the side of the Central Powers.

The Federal Assembly had not only been debating the appointment of the General in Chief. They also granted the Federal Council unlimited plenary powers. These allowed the government to take whatever measures it considered necessary to uphold 'Switzerland's security, integrity and neutrality'. Although not all enacted immediately, these measures would prove far-reaching, often unpopular and impact upon all forms of life, even the most mundane. One of the simple freedoms that would come under attack – and one which most people take for granted until it is removed, was the 'sacred bond' that existed between letter writers and the Post Office as the government insisted that letters could be opened and nothing that La Poste could say altered this decree. Opened letters in Régina's files demonstrate that her correspondence had become the subject of scrutiny.

Almost immediately those who were dubious about Wille's unbiased sentiments were proved correct. On 1 September, he wrote to his German-born wife assuring her that his 'whole heart was with Germany'. Even allowing for this being private correspondence, it indicates a distinct lack of neutrality on behalf of the leader of the army of a country desperate to preserve its neutrality. This was not his only questionable pronouncement. On 20 July 1915, he wrote to the Federal Council suggesting that Switzerland should enter the war on the German side, a suggestion repeated in March

1916 – to the outrage of predominantly, but far from exclusively, Western Switzerland. Perhaps Régina and the many other individuals recruited by the Central Powers in Switzerland felt that siding with Germany was simply aligning themselves with the 'correct' side.

The Call to Arms Swiss style and the Call to Foreign Arms in Switzerland

In 1817, following the end of the Napoleonic wars, the Swiss army underwent reorganisation. Although it was occasionally tweaked, and a certain amount of what was dubbed 'Prussianization' occurred (although not sufficient to satisfy Ulrich Wille), the model was still in place in August 1914 (as it is to this day). Unlike most other countries with universal male conscription, the Swiss 'Citizen Army' is different: rather than spending typically three or four years with the colours, following initial training, every Swiss male aged between 18 and 48 (increased to 60 in a serious threat to Swiss neutrality) serves for short periods of time every year. Now, with a genuine and continuing fear that either France or Germany might invade Swiss territory to try to outflank their opponent's line, the country was facing a National Emergency.

The rapid mobilisation of some 220,000 men and 45,000 horses affected the entire Swiss population. As in belligerent countries, families flocked to the stations to bid loved ones farewell. August Fontolliet, 13 years old and from Nyon on Lake Geneva (Lac Léman to francophone Swiss), just 10kms from the French border, had been busy documenting events since the assassination of the Archduke. In his preserved notebook, *Carnet de Guerre*, he noted on 2 August how his father, a bank employee, 'left for the war (Papa part en guerre)'. An acute observer of events and an avid newspaper reader, he also excitedly noted on 4 August the first of the countless spy stories that would feature in the Swiss press. Few citizens at this point realized how many salvos from the spy war were already being fired from within their territory.

Every student of the Western Front knows that the trenches 'stretched from the North Sea to the Swiss border'. Less well known is that even before Germany declared war on France and as the Swiss Army mustered, the first two Franco-German fatalities occurred at Jonchérey a few kilometres from the Swiss border, an area now lovingly restored and referred to as 'Kilometre 0', where the then French, German and Swiss borders met. Here, the Swiss border guards could look into the eyes of German soldiers on one side and French ones on the other – and at times fraternise with both. On 2 August, 21-year-old French Caporal Jules Peugeot and 22-year-old German Lieutenant Albert Mayer exchanged fire, killing each other. (Both young men are now honoured by their respective sides as their country's first casualty.) Demonstrating the truth behind the statement to the victor the laurels, Peugeot is remembered by an elaborate memorial in Jonchérey, Mayer's grave just one of hundreds in the nearby German military cemetery in Illfurth, Alsace, an area which to him was German and is now, once again, French. These contrasting memorials resemble those awarded to spies. Some, such as Louise de Bettignies who acted for the 'winning' side, had statues erected to them; the mortal remains and often the names of those who, like Régina Diana, gathered intelligence for the vanquished, almost erased from history. Mayer and Peugeot's deaths made it uncomfortably apparent to the Swiss that this war was being waged, quite literally, within their earshot and eyesight, as it would continue to be for the next four years. Switzerland herself soon had her first 'war' casualties; by 27 August some forty-two Swiss soldiers had lost their lives: five from sunstroke, five 'delirious' cases, six suicides, twelve accidents and twelve from sickness. (August Fontolliet)

In August 1914, General Wille had 218,000 Swiss men aged between 18 and 48 under his command (with reserves of another 200,00 available). Once it became apparent that Switzerland was not, imminently at least, about to suffer Belgium's fate, the numbers guarding the frontiers were reduced. As Jonathan Steinberg points out, 'To maintain an army of 250,000 men in varying degrees of readiness out of a total population of about 3 million required an immense effort', not to mention sacrifice on the part of their families at home. According to Jean-Jacques Langendorf, these men became ever more demoralised as the sufferings of their families at home increased. Men in the military served on average for 500 days, generally far from their homes. While in terms of countries at war, this is relatively few, Swiss society was ill-prepared for such an exodus of men and struggled to cope with the social ramifications and eventually unrest. Despite, according to the same source, Swiss 'borders being violated around 1,000 times and Swiss airspace around 800 times', the men became increasingly bored and disaffected throughout a war that was impacting – for the majority of them negatively, upon every aspect of their emotional and financial lives.

It was not only Swiss men who were called to arms. From the beginning of August, the Swiss press carried frequent announcements in a variety of languages summoning foreign males back to their own native land.

French, Austrian, German, Russian, Montenegrin and Serbian men were amongst those who were instructed to return home – and transport was provided to ensure that they had no excuse for not presenting themselves on the required day. Some authorities put the numbers of returnees at some 200,000, 'leading [unusually for Switzerland!] to chaos in the trains and border stations and posing considerable problems for the Swiss economy,' as well as for the authorities trying to check on the legitimacy of those rushing hither and thither across Switzerland. There were several newspaper reports of 'spies' at the stations. As Vuilleumier and other Swiss historians note, 10,000 Frenchmen living in Geneva – whose population in 1914 was 139,500, quickly returned to France – 7,000 of them never to return. Many Swiss cantons experienced an unprecedented exodus. In the reverse direction, while some Swiss men returned from abroad to fulfil their duties under the Swiss colours, many Swiss families continued to live abroad – 2,000 of them in Paris. Some soon experienced genuine hardship, even turning to soup kitchens to avoid starvation. So many Swiss citizens living in major French cities made it easy for others who were (or appeared to be) Swiss to pass almost unnoticed in areas they might be sent to infiltrate for less legitimate reasons. No one would have paid any attention to the milliner working as première chapelière at Mme Lelavandier's and covertly spying upon the officers at the Chateau de Vincennes. Similarly, when she lived for longer periods in Marseille, the singer Régina Diana would have been just one more woman walking the boards to eke out a living.

Yet another group of men deserted Switzerland's towns and villages. Vuilleumier argues that, like their counterparts across Europe, a number of young Swiss imagined there was a glamour in fighting on foreign fields; while those already resident abroad enlisted with the colours of their host country, others took the active decision of crossing Switzerland's borders to enlist. There are examples of Swiss men in the German, and even in isolated incidents, the Russian Armies. The majority however served in the Régiment de Marche de la Légion Etrangère (French Foreign Legion) – the Legion's very existence facilitated the entry of foreign men to it ranks. The *Swiss Historical Dictionary* believes that around 14,000 Swiss volunteers (a figure contested by another historian as being too high – 6,000 is her estimate) were Légionnaires and there are even estimates that around 3,000 Swiss fought with the French at Gallipoli. Some were killed, including the son of the Swiss Consul in Marseille on 27 September 1916. Beyond the ease with which they could enlist in the Foreign Legion, the question of why so many young Swiss (accurate statistics regarding their linguistic background have not been traced although in 1916 the President of the *Comité des suisses au service de la France* mentioned having been in contact with 500 francophone and 300 germanophone soldiers) chose to serve with the French was answered at a banquet held in Paris on Swiss National Day, 1 August 1918. A Swiss captain serving with the Légion simply stated: 'If Germany wins this war, Switzerland will be wiped from the face of the earth'.

By 1915, worried by the drain of its young men and perhaps also with an eye on the issue of neutrality, which was questioned in an article in a Munich paper asking if Switzerland were truly neutral, the Swiss government took steps to ban the practice of enlisting in foreign armies (this only became law in 1927). What the Munich report (quoted by the *Gazette de Lausanne* on 12 August 1918) naturally drew a veil over was the other, arguably more effective, way in which both Swiss nationals and foreign residents, including (currently unbeknownst to any but a select group of insiders) one from Geneva, were serving the German military cause.

War on the Newspaper Front

From the opening days, it became apparent that newspapers were exploiting the rift that was rapidly opening between Switzerland's linguistic groups. The francophone press went so far as to refer to the German invaders of Belgium as 'Boches' or 'Huns', negative terminology which encouraged many French-speaking Swiss to feel that their government had not protested loudly enough at Germany's aggressive actions. This view differed from that held by several germanophone newspapers, and, as Belgian refugees began flocking into Switzerland, the Bern newspaper *Berner Tagblatt* even advised them to go home, where 'under sensible German administration, they could work on getting the situation back to normal'. Whilst the 25 August 1914 *Journal de Genève* reported the destruction of the world-famous library in the Belgian city of Louvain as a 'barbaric act', not all Swiss newspapers were outraged. The influential *Neues Zürcher Zeitung* only 'assumed' this to have occurred and portrayed the German Army as defending itself against the guerrilla Belgians. Many French-speaking Swiss felt that the Germanic press had done nothing to express outrage at the treatment meted out to Belgians by the aggressors. On 27–28 September 1914, a week after the bombardment of Reims Cathedral, another Geneva paper, the *Tribune de Genève* opened its columns to a public protest which lasted twelve days – significantly, protests were received from both sides of the linguistic divide. That the Swiss Government again did nothing to register official protests at this latest outrages, stoked the idea that the Federal Council (if not the whole Swiss body politic), as well as General Wille, were Kaiser's men.

At times, the Swiss government struggled to control the press and although some journalists did maintain a scrupulous neutrality, others were considered 'enragés' [fully engaged] and their views cannot fail to have affected those who read them; many newspapers published two or three editions daily indicating that the readership was wide. A modern article in one of the key Swiss history websites for this period, www.1914–1918.ch, argues that a number of germanophone newspapers were often edited and even funded by Germany, consequently the Swiss German press gives a less than accurate representation of the views of 'ordinary' Swiss Germans (and indeed parliamentarians) who were far more neutral than their papers suggest, and were not all holding their breath awaiting a German victory.

In addition to the many newspapers published in all major Swiss towns, copies of belligerent countries' newspapers were available to purchase. Anyone living in Switzerland could read for themselves how both sides were presenting events; belligerent powers acquired their opponents' newspapers via neutral countries. Although these national papers were heavily censored, local ones, which also found their way into Switzerland, were subject to less scrutiny. Fritz-Karl Roegels noted that even announcements in the small ads columns could yield a gold mine of information to agents embarking upon missions. Spies working abroad were also told to scour their local press and forward on various snippets which could be pieced together reveal a 'bigger picture'. Spymasters in Switzerland would place small ads in Swiss newspapers sold abroad; an innocent-seeming insertion could reveal the date or time an agent was to report back to Switzerland, or who would meet them at the station; certainly when in Paris, with its large immigrant Swiss community and thus francophone Swiss newspapers, Régina may have received messages this way. While letters were increasingly subject to censorship and inevitable delays, such a ruse would pass undetected. Even when French censorship began to ban small ads appearing in their own papers it did not extend this ban to neutral papers sold in France.

Swiss correspondents were also working in foreign capitals and hubs and Swiss newspapers carried reports from both sides as well as from the big press agencies, British Reuters, German Wolff and French Havas. Du Bois argues that Swiss German newspapers seem only to have taken seriously dispatches from Wolff, discounting those of the French agency Havas (which broke the news of Régina's fate) as half-truths or even lies. The word

Havas even passed temporarily into Swiss-German meaning to 'be economical with the truth'.

The Swiss Government soon kept a weather eye on the Swiss press. Aware that supposed cultural divisions and biased reporting could tear Switzerland apart not to mention jeopardise its neutral status, the government warned the press that articles appearing to favour one or other belligerent could lead to a paper's suspension for the duration of hostilities. Journalists from all linguistic areas were reminded of their duty to be neutral and should not attempt to influence public opinion. The extent to which they succeeded (or even wished to succeed) is open to question.

In October 1914, the government suspended two francophone newspapers and cautioned five others for attitudes potentially prejudicial to Swiss neutrality. An article published in the *Gazette de Lausanne* under the heading 'sanitisation of the press' 'assainissement de la presse' reported that the satirical *Guguss*, published in Geneva and widely distributed there and in the adjacent canton of Vaud and already renowned for its anti-Kaiser message and cartoons and its obvious sympathy with the treatment meted out to Belgian civilians (19 September 1914 features a cartoon of a Belgian infant brutally held aloft on a German bayonet), was banned 'for the duration'. Swiss federal archives reveal that the decision, taken at the highest level on 7 October 1914, stemmed from the belief that *Guguss* risked compromising Swiss relations with a 'foreign state' (which some readers interpreted as meaning Germany) and consequently threatened Swiss neutrality. Its reappearance under a different title was also forbidden (although it did reappear as *Le Petit Suisse)*. Anyone who edited, printed, or sold the paper would face a military tribunal, Swiss neutrality being a military not a civil issue. Some Geneva residents might have seen the actions taken against *Guguss* (and subsequently those taken against the Lausanne newspaper *Le Clairon* for its anti-German reporting) as indicating that anti-German sentiments were unacceptable to the Swiss authorities, particularly as the German language *Schaffhauser Zeitung* was only reprimanded for publishing articles that were seen as inflammatory towards 'foreign' governments. In none of these cases, nor others that followed, was it stated which the 'foreign governments' were but it is safe to assume that they followed linguistic lines.

A fierce battle was waged on the newspaper front during the opening months of the war, and not only within Switzerland. Berlin went so far as to accuse the Swiss francophone press of being financed and sustained by French and Monegasque funds, accusations which Edouard Secrétan, the widely respected *Gazette de Lausanne* editor, termed 'calumnies'. On 15

October 1914, he was heartened by the support shown by the Swiss German language newspaper *Solothurner Zeitung*,which admitted that although Swiss sentiments were divided, Swiss German reporters were outraged by such accusations and that '*Swiss*' [sic] journalists, working for a free press, were entitled, and had the right, to publish their own opinions.

Despite its accusations, the Reich was not averse to trying to tweak Swiss francophone opinion via the press. Although not always successful, the views aired may have influenced citizens struggling to decide where their loyalties lay. One paper *Le Nouvelliste,* was even founded in Geneva to 'disseminate the German truth'. Some outraged residents took action against its vendors, tearing the papers from them and throwing them in the gutter. While regretting such incidents, the 8 October 1914 *Gazette de Lausanne* argued that this 'pan-germanist' newspaper's proprietors only had themselves to thank. *Le Nouvelliste* was undoubtedly far from a unique example of newspapers fighting for and influencing 'hearts and minds' across the linguistic divide.

It is tempting to believe that the German legation in Bern was behind this publication. Although the name of the paper is changed to *Paris-Express* it is probable that Léon Labarre, author of the sensational, fictional but with many grains of truth, *L'Espionnage Boche en Suisse* is referring to *Le Nouvelliste* when he implies that the paper was instigated at the behest of German military attaché, Major Busso von Bismarck. Labarre is in no doubt that one of the legation's aims was to disseminate what he calls the 'German truth' in francophone Switzerland.

It was not only the Swiss and international newspapers who fought for the emotional allegiance of the Swiss population – and sometimes for more than just hearts and minds. So too did the spymasters and recruiters who, even pre-war, had flocked into the country on behalf of all the Great Powers. Perhaps what the Swiss authorities did not fully realise at this early juncture was just how quickly and continuously the intelligence services from the main belligerents would raise the stakes in the games they were playing in this tiny, neutral haven. They were about to face a steep learning curve. Janet Morgan confirms that 'all the belligerents ran secret services in Switzerland; all energetically denied it'. In this outwardly peaceful little paradise, 'in hotels and restaurants, on trams, trains and omnibuses, on the steamers plying the lakes, in shops, stations and post offices, someone was always watching', but not as carefully as they should have been for Switzerland would become a den of spies and this, more than any article published in any newspaper of any leaning, threatened the neutrality that the army had been mobilised to defend on Swiss National day, 1 August 1914.

Chapter 6

Switzerland: The Nest of Spies

If they so wished, Swiss males could join the French Foreign Legion, but there were few ways in which Swiss nationals or residents with pro-German leanings could enlist in the German Army. One form of service that was open to both genders however, although strictly illegal due to Switzerland's fragile neutral status, was espionage. To better understand Régina and the stories of other Swiss spies it is worth examining Switzerland's stance on spies, both in theory and in practice, as well as the all-pervading spy fever. Cultural and military attachés, recruiters, as well as putative spies were all key players in the spy operations run out of Switzerland. These both form the backdrop to and explain Régina's story, and shed light on the depth of her involvement in this undercover world for which she had been groomed since 1910.

To spy or not to spy

Anticipating Swiss neutrality in any future conflict, foreign secret services had long been on the lookout for potential recruiters and spies; they had infiltrated Switzerland, aiming to be in prime position if and when hostilities broke out. For their part, the Swiss government appeared to be leaving nothing to chance, and, once war had been declared, politicians (optimistically) announced that in line with its position of neutrality, any Secret Service from any country was forbidden to operate on Swiss soil. However, as Laird Easton, editor of the diaries of Count von Kessler (German cultural attaché in Bern from 1916–1918) notes, while being an island of peace and relative prosperity amid the bloodshed that engulfed Europe, Switzerland was a cockpit of intrigue, secret negotiations and espionage – it had long been so. Régina's 'recruitment' in 1910 and subsequent pre-war deployment is undoubtedly not a unique example.

Should anyone be under any illusions as to the seriousness of their intentions, the Swiss Federal Council stipulated that any foreign intelligence service garnering and disseminating information through Switzerland would be subject to the full force of the law. Telegrams and telephone offices, apart from communications sent by and received in embassies, were placed under surveillance, actions that would make the role of military attachés attached to diplomatic missions, increasingly important. However, as the 'full force of the law' amounted to little more than a short term of imprisonment and a fine that many Swiss themselves considered derisory, none of the main belligerents heeded these pronouncements. With few disincentives, spy rings, spymasters and recruiters proliferated – as did the public's appetite for spy stories as a quick trawl through the two main French language newspapers *Gazette de Lausanne* and *Journal de Genève* demonstrates.

On 3 August 1914, the *Gazette de Lausanne* reported its first spy story: eight French agents had been apprehended in Basel along with several carrier pigeons. The paper warned people to be on the alert and guard their tongues as spies might be listening and reminded readers that the presence of spies could jeopardise Switzerland's neutral status; nine days later, the paper revealed that a significant number of spies were living in the country. From this point on there are well over 500 references to spies in this highly respected and widely read Swiss francophone paper whose editor Edouard Secrétan could never have been accused of being a sensationalist. Spies and their treatment would remain a 'hot topic' throughout and beyond the war with both sides accusing Switzerland (with some justification) of being the 'Promised Land' ('Terre Bénie') for spies.

Spy fever was confined neither to the early months of the war, nor to the *Gazette de Lausanne*. While newspapers pandered to readers' desires for spy stories, some organisations worried about the negative social impact of the supposed glamour of spying, particularly on vulnerable young working-class females – the very class from which Régina had been recruited. In the 2 October 1915 *Journal de Genève*, the Union Internationale des Amies pleaded with young women to resist the lure of financial gain and refuse to be sucked into involvement in espionage. It assured those who were down on their luck – or indeed facing penury – that such work would both place them in considerable danger and sully their reputation. Having assured would-be spies that the work was dangerous and unglamorous, it does not seem to have suggested other suitable employment.

This organisation may have been fighting a losing battle in terms of remuneration versus risk. On 23 November 1915, the *Journal de Genève* carried news of the arrest in Geneva of Marie-Thérèse Le Philipponat, a 32-year-old Frenchwoman from the Lille area (occupied by Germany since 12 October 1914). She had been addressing letters to two fictitious gentlemen, one at a hotel in Geneva, the other in Zurich – ploys Régina also used.

When subject to tests, invisible ink revealed a wealth of information about Belgian and French troop movements. She had earned some 4,000 francs (even today a very substantial sum) for her endeavours. A German lieutenant collected some of her letters from Geneva, the hotelier himself forwarded on others to Zurich. All ended up in Germany. During the case, she told the court that the Germans had coerced her into becoming a spy. After intensive training in Antwerp she had been sent back into France. Found guilty she was sentenced to eight months in prison and a 2,000 francs fine – hardly a deterrent to those working for the well-funded German Secret Service. Just the following day, the *Gazette de Lausanne* reported that a military tribunal in Zurich had condemned a ring of German recruiters charged with ensnaring francophone spies. The proposed remuneration, between 500 and 2,000 francs per mission, would have seemed riches to those who were already struggling to make ends meet due to the rampant inflation from which Switzerland was far from protected. There is ample evidence in the stories of Régina and other spies that there was good money to be made for those prepared to take the risk.

Those who did not wish to chance their luck with real spying could at least watch it on stage. In Lausanne, in November 1915 a popular play entitled *L'Espionne* (the Female Spy) had its run lengthened by popular demand; it transferred to Geneva where additional reduced seats were available for children and on Sundays. Spy-crazy children could do more than go to the theatre. An English spy story was translated into French and serialised for younger readers in the *Gazette de Lausanne* in February 1916.

If spy fever was now part of the Swiss air, New Year 1916 saw no let-up in newspapers informing readers about arrests. On 3 January 1916, the *Journal de Genève* reported that a Swiss woman had been fined 400 francs for placing small advertisements recruiting agents to spy for Germany in Italy, who had entered the war on the side of the Entente Cordiale in May 1915 (Switzerland now had a belligerent on all of its borders). The 22 February *Gazette de Lausanne* reported on a German recruiter who had sent a woman euphemistically referred to as a Parisian 'demi-mondaine' to Geneva to act as his intermediary – perhaps to perform in one of the city's many café-concerts, places of low/middle-brow entertainment to which, as we shall see in Chapter 7 those from all walks of life flocked.

This 22 February story increases understanding not only of Régina, but also of the world of the working-class (female) spies and their role in intelligence gathering. Placing recruiters and informers in border areas was a useful strategy; the population was often transient with civilians not to mention deserters from all armies endeavouring to enter Switzerland via its many, often unmanned, porous and indeed unlikely entry points. A much-used village café in La Cure in the Jura region about 44 kilometres from Geneva had (and still has) one door in France and another in Switzerland, neither of which appears to have been guarded. Irrespective of the route they had used, deserters who had successfully reached Switzerland from France (or indeed Germany) were milked for information about the side they had abandoned and on occasion 'turned' and sent back to act as an informer. As more than one spymaster, including Régina's handlers, commented, individual items of information which on their own might amount to little can, when placed alongside other snippets, build up a vital picture. 'Demi-mondaines' and music-hall artistes such as Régina could easily glean useful information from deserters and other escapees who would have been likely to find their way to crowded places such as cafés where they could mingle with the crowds and drown their sorrows amongst friendly female company. And those like Régina who were already established performers in café-concerts would have been and remained especially valuable to spymasters seeking information.

By February 1916, the Swiss authorities had had enough of these activities, which were endangering their country's neutral status. They announced that all foreign agents would be expelled – not that this appears to have been either successful or strictly implemented. Furthermore, most espionage cases would now be tried by civil (as opposed to the previous military) courts and harsher penalties imposed, although there is little evidence of this. According to the 29 February 1916 *Gazette de Lausanne*, one Colonel Egli, himself deeply implicated in spying, believed that whenever a spy trial was reported in the press, rather than acting as a deterrent, the number of 'wannabe' spies increased.

From 1917 a sensationalist weekly series, *Collection Patrie*, was published in France retelling in dramatic terms, glorious moments of wartime derring-do based, often loosely, on actual events but told with a distinctly germanophobe slant; the series continued post-war running to 154 episodes until the public tired of it. In number 138 *L'espionnage boche en Suisse*, Léon Labarre bases his account of German spying in Switzerland on a German recruiter who 'pimps' for vulnerable, rather stupid artistes in a Geneva café-concert as well as in comfortable cafés on the edge of the lake. However sensationalist the story, it contains several grains of truth that can be placed alongside more reliable sources of record, some almost seem to be based on Régina's own story. The first page asserts that the German legation in

Bern was funding what Labarre terms 'repugnant sneaks' (mouchards). Disregarding the ins and outs of the trite little story, what is of interest is the extent to which the supposedly covert activities of the correctly named military attaché 'Major von Bismarck' and his ambassador Baron von Romberg, appear to have been known.

Irrespective of the measures that the authorities were trying to take and of which Swiss citizens were generally in favour, David Auberson argues that France and Germany had no intention of refraining from turning Switzerland into the main theatre of the 'shadow war' (la guerre des ombres). The *Journal de Genève* would have agreed, a front-page article (2 April 1916) argued that the battle of the spies was being waged on Swiss territory. Unbeknownst to the journalist, the battle had another two and a half years to run. The official post-war figures undoubtedly reveal but the tip of a forever-submerged iceberg. Two hundred agents working for France were arrested in Switzerland between 1914 and 1918; a significant number of German agents were arrested and not infrequently executed in France, while as early as 1915, a network of 120 individuals working for Germany had been dismantled and, as Régina's story shows, there were numerous others.

The derisory sentences that the Swiss courts continued to pass on those who were caught – often little more than a few months' imprisonment and a small fine (according to reports in the *Gazette de Lausanne*, which reported on many of the trials, women got off even more lightly than men). Writing in 1934, the German Military Attaché in Bern, Busso von Bismarck, believed that, with the rising cost of living, spying was an easy and financially attractive option for those who had fallen on hard financial times. Jean-Jacques Langendorff calculated that food inflation was 145 per cent; 100kg of potatoes, which would have cost 12.50 francs in April 1914, had rocketed to 27 francs by December 1918. Men serving in the army received minimal financial compensation (only 1.30 francs a day), often leaving their families impoverished. Desperate women queued for hours to buy food with the government seemingly unable to step in and alleviate the problem; this led to very significant social unrest, which reached its peak in the closing months of 1918. Meanwhile, many working in the pre-war booming tourist entertainment and luxury goods industries lost their jobs, although previous precision factories such as watchmaking, metal and machine industries turned themselves over to munitions – which they legitimately supplied to both sides, often from the same factories. Bismarck felt that for those who were not facing financial distress, there was some perceived glamour attached to spying and there were plenty of recruiters ready to ensnare them.

One group of potential agents who particularly interested recruiters were foreign nationals with residency rights in Switzerland; this made travel in and out of Switzerland easy. To further assist recruiters, the Swiss police seemed relatively uninterested in these residents' activities. However, this had a negative side for residents arrested abroad for spying. Arguably because they would have had little or no leverage, the Swiss government appears to have abandoned these individuals to their fate whereas they did, on occasion, intervene on behalf of Swiss nationals (more successfully for women). Lausanne and Geneva newspapers reported the overturning of the sentence passed on Mlle Zemp following a Swiss governmental appeal. Stemming from the Zemp case, the influential German-language newspaper, *Neues Zürcher Zeitung* believed that Swiss Germans living in France were under immediate suspicion of espionage irrespective of the legitimacy of their activities. But as French-speaking Swiss living in France blended in with the local population, those who, like Régina, spied for Germany could pass undetected. The larger the city, the more transient the population, the greater the invisibility.

The Swiss civil and military authorities were painfully aware that the Confederation was being turned into, and indeed remained, a nest of spies. In a report submitted to General Ulrich Wille in 1919, Theophil Sprecher von Bernegg, Chief of the [Swiss] General Staff, regretfully admitted that 'we were never able successfully to combat nor repress espionage'. However, while the activities of foreign spies may have threatened Swiss neutrality, they did not seemingly jeopardise Swiss military activities or secrets. Bernegg felt that the military hierarchy were thus either uninterested, or less interested than they should have been, in the actions of foreign Intelligence Services operating within Switzerland. He also concluded that the Swiss structure of both federal and cantonal police hindered anti-espionage work; historian Auberson places at least some blame on magistrates and police turning a blind eye when spies for their preferred side were known to be active. Border police and customs officers were not infrequently in the pay of one or the other of the Secret Services, even both simultaneously. A prime example of this, reported in *Gazette de Lausanne* on 30 January 1917, was the arrest of Dépassel, the Brigadier of the Geneva Police, who, despite overseeing 'spy surveillance', was accused of acting for both sides at once. Having disappeared from Geneva, he was condemned in absentia to five years in prison and a 1,000 franc fine. A co-defendant, a more junior officer from the canton of Vaud, received a lesser custodial sentence and reduced fine.

With the passing of time, this view of Switzerland as a haven for spies did not alter. Modern historians continue to agree with Oscar Ray of the French Intelligence Service who commented that Switzerland was the 'promised land' (terre bénie) for spies; a similar point was made albeit more prosaically by the French authorities who gathered the evidence against Régina. Even allowing for Ray's purple prose and exaggerations, there is undoubtedly more than a grain of truth in his assertion that, if not, as he claims, 'every', then certainly 'some hotel porter[s], café waiter[s], chauffeur[s] and groom[s] worked for one or the other Intelligence Service – and often both at the same time'. Once again, such individuals feature in Régina's story.

In 1936, with storm clouds again gathering over Europe, Emile Thilo, an expert on Swiss jurisprudence – especially espionage – scathingly commented that penalties imposed by federal courts were no deterrent; he argued that the Swiss authorities had turned a blind eye to spies who had swarmed across Switzerland, and to the machinations of those who recruited them, some of whom came close to breaking, or even broke, the diplomatic code.

'Our Man in ...'

By 1914, many of the main belligerents were already positioned in embassies in Switzerland, their networks awaiting war's starting pistol. Despite the Swiss government's efforts (which many felt were not energetic enough to counter the ploys of various intelligence agencies), their operations would continue until the bitter end.

Turning first to France's 'man in Bern', military attaché Gaston Pageot created a wide-reaching, generally efficient network with tentacles spreading across the whole of Switzerland. Christophe Vuilleumier argues that, in anticipation of hostilities breaking out and with Switzerland likely to be pro-Germany, France had embedded a captain Larguier in their Embassy. He had established an outpost in Geneva with agents placed within the police force, indicating that the aforementioned Dépassel and his co-defendant were far from unique, and proving the accuracy of von Bismarck's cynical remark that 'anyone can be corrupted if the price is right.' Meanwhile, Lieutenant-Colonel Parchet developed intelligence centres in Basel and Zurich, in the border town of Pontarlier as well as in Evian (on the French side of Lake Geneva) and in Annemasse, the nearby Franco-Swiss border town. Parchet even successfully infiltrated the German Service with an informer who relayed vital, reliable information to military attaché Pageot. The French appear to have been successful in recruiting potential agents amongst the refugees flocking into Switzerland from Belgium, Occupied France, and the battle-torn areas of Northern France from which all civilians had been evacuated. To add to the pool of potential recruits whom the French were keeping within their sights, many (initially) affluent refugees had settled in the francophone lakeside towns of Geneva, Lausanne, Vevey and Montreux. According to Phillipe Valode, as these individuals' money began to disappear, and with no hope of increasing their funds, some women at least faced a choice between prostitution or spying and there were plenty of potential recruiters to assist them make their choice.

The British diplomatic set-up was, in the early days at least, woefully inadequate and never appears to have caught up. Major Walter Kirke, a key player in British Intelligence in Paris and himself a successful spymaster, recognised that military attachés were ideally placed to identify potential agents and informers and there is no reason to believe that the British willingly refrained from so doing in neutral countries. However, the British operation in Switzerland got off to a disastrous start and never achieved the level of efficiency of either their enemies or allies in Bern or any other part of the confederation. At one point, the British intelligence operation in the Swiss capital consisted of a meteorologist who climbed mountains twice a day to report on wind speed to assist flight planning and operations involving gas! To further compound British inefficiencies, in the early years, the (non-British) Consul and pro-Consul in the British Consulate in Geneva were almost certainly German informers who tried to lure British agents based on the French side of Lake Geneva across to Switzerland where they could be arrested. In 1916, Kirke washed his hands of them all, believing 'this Swiss show is a waste of money'.

On 16 April 1916, the *Gazette de Lausanne* reviewed *The Secrets of the German War Office.* Published in England on 7 August 1914, the author, Armgaard Karl Graves was an arguably ineffective, allegedly Swiss-born 'spy', who worked for the Kaiser in Edinburgh in the 1910s where he was soon rumbled. He claimed that the German espionage system was indubitably the best organised and funded. His comment about the eclectic social backgrounds of its spies: 'princes, counts, doctors, lawyers, mondaines of the great world, demi-mondaines of the half-world', not to mention 'singers, dancers, and artists', certainly contains several grains of truth. He added that female agents needed to possess charm, beauty, tact, know how to act like a lady, and be at ease in the wider world. For those with these accomplishments, the pay was good. Régina, as the postcards written to her by her military admirers confirm, ticked all these boxes.

Partly contradicting Graves, several of the German and Austrian contributors to two volumes relating to German wartime intelligence activities (*Espionnage Contre-Espionnage)* stress that Germany was 'too moral' a nation to stoop to acquiring information about the enemy through espionage. Morality may have had less to do with this supposed nineteenth century tardiness than the theories of the great German military theorist Carl von Clausewitz (1780–1831). His *On War* was widely studied in staff colleges in the late nineteenth century, and having seen the ineffectiveness of Prussian intelligence during the Napoleonic Wars, he concluded in his very brief Chapter VI, 'Information in War', that a 'great part of the information obtained in War is contradictory, a still greater part is false, and by far the greatest part is of a doubtful character'.

Whatever von Clausewitz's views, in the years immediately preceding the First World War, Germany had been making up for her supposedly tardy arrival in this world of subterfuge. By 1914, she had seventeen military and eight naval attachés placed in embassies around the world. Like their counterparts of all nationalities, they were responsible to, and attached to, the German diplomatic corps of the country in which they were serving. Their duty was to report to the local ambassador who in turn sent dispatches back to the German Foreign Office in Berlin and thence to the General Staff. All attachés and diplomatic staff were subject to strict rules of conduct for gleaning information: newspapers, military journals, diplomatic conversations and military manoeuvres to which they were invited were legitimate, but overt espionage was (supposedly) frowned upon. Once war had started, neutral America inflicted heavy penalties on attachés who did not abide by the rules. According to Markus Pöhlmann, the German military and naval attachés in Washington became so deeply involved in espionage and covert action that in late 1915 they were officially requested to leave. The Swiss were less stringent in their approach.

There were three significant players in the German Embassy in Bern. The highest placed was the Ambassador Baron Gisbert von Romberg. American attaché in Paris, Eric Fisher Wood, saw Romberg as 'very impressive and keen of mind'. There is documentary evidence that von Romberg was sailing close to the wind in terms of diplomacy. His report to von Bethmann Hollweg, the German Chancellor, on 29 September 1914 and quoted by Jonathan Steinberg shows how his close involvement in intelligence gathering,

> *From the very first day since the outbreak of war Switzerland has discreetly placed at our disposal her entire secret military intelligence*

> *service. They give us information about intercepted cables, which might be useful, and more important news from their overseas representatives.*

Von Romberg's friend, cultural attaché Count Harry Kessler (of Irish/German descent), was based at the embassy in Bern from late summer 1916. His official brief was to organise German cultural propaganda in Switzerland and promote the German point of view to the Swiss population. He and his superiors believed that neutral Switzerland represented Germany's best chance of counteracting what they considered to be Allied wilful misrepresentation and propaganda directed against the 'brutal Hun', noting in in his diary 11 September 1916 that Switzerland had been,

> *flooded by the Entente with cultural propaganda of every kind, travelling lectures, theatre, coquettes, bribery. Everywhere one feels subterranean forces at work that will one day blow up.*

One hundred years later, evidence of this so-called 'flood' has proved elusive.

Using numerous contacts in the highest echelons of German culture, and a generous budget, Kessler was soon bringing German orchestras, theatre groups and art exhibitions to Switzerland. Films were commissioned for those preferring middlebrow culture and Kessler was to ensure that these 'were screened in all cinemas'. Every corner of Switzerland, every remote cinema, as well as those in the large towns, was to be 'penetrated' (2 October 1916). The ambitious Régina nursed high hopes of a cinema career, was this part of the package offered to her? This blanket propaganda aimed to counter any possible belief that Germany and her allies were in any way 'finished' and remind the Swiss that their German neighbours were eager to share their enviable reputation for Kultur with their co-linguists. German General Ludendorff feeling that Kessler's task was 'of the utmost importance', Germany invested considerable sums in these initiatives. On 25 October 1916, the ambassador approved his request for 1.25 million Swiss francs for so-called 'cultural propaganda' to be spent up to 1 July 1917. One can only speculate upon the extent to which the campaign may have won the hearts and minds of individuals and made them open to approaches by recruiters to the German cause.

But the German Embassy in Bern was involved in far more than promoting a cosy Germano-Swiss cultural relationship. The key figure was their long-standing Military attaché Busso von Bismarck who in 1909 had proved his worth when he had concluded an intelligence-sharing deal with the

Swiss Chief of Military Intelligence, Friedrich von Wattenwyl. According to Jefferson Adams, 'a profuse exchange of high-level information concerning Great Britain, France and Russia soon resulted'. The Bern Embassy was considered so crucial to German espionage operations that, despite having only a skeleton staff when he was originally appointed, by 1918 Bismarck had eighty people working for him. His contribution to *Espionnage Contre-Espionnage* provides copious information about his methods and undoubted enthusiasm for the job, enthusiasm so great that Lieutenant-Colonel Walter Nicolaï, chief of the German Military Intelligence (*Abteilung IIIb)*, warned him at one point that he was in danger of compromising the Embassy. An accurate conclusion as we shall see. Keen to stress his own innocence, Bismarck himself felt that along with his counterpart in Madrid, he became the target of an Allied disinformation campaign.

German nationals living in Switzerland (some six per cent of the total population) and pro-German Swiss were keen to share what Bismarck called a 'torrent of information' with him. In testimony to Swiss precision, he found Swiss informers particularly reliable. Almost certainly on his orders, the German consulate in Basel provided both French and German passports for agents working in France on Germany's behalf. These documents allowed them to spy in France, to travel freely through Switzerland and onwards to Germany without arousing suspicion, and personally deliver information to handlers in Germany. In Bismarck's defence, there is firm evidence that all belligerents used their consulates in neutral territory to this end.

Bismarck had cultivated close personal relationships with members of the Swiss Army's High Command – with whom he claims to have had almost daily contact; his links of kinship with General of Switzerland Ulrich Wille also worked in his favour. The predominance of 'Prussianised' germanophone Regular Army officers, a number of whom, like the head of the Canton of Bern's Military Department Karl Scheuer, believed 'a German victory is desirable', and according to the 'many Swiss officers, blinded by their Prussian sympathies, expected gross violations of their neutrality to come from the French side only', meant that Bismarck was pushing at an open door. Despite his eagerness to promote the German cause and garner information about Germany's enemies to forward to the Fatherland, Bismarck remained aware of the need to preserve Switzerland's neutral status; less, it should be said, out of finer feelings and more because it protected Southern Germany and the German Army's left wing.

If Bismarck was keen to protect the German left wing, the Swiss Government was trying to protect the country's neutral status and, according to Vuilleumier in April 1918, sent a reminder (not for the first time) to consulates of all belligerent countries that it behoved them to respect Swiss laws regarding visas, residency permits and right of entry to Switzerland, and warned that any consul not obeying the law would be subject to the full weight of Swiss justice. This, the reminder added, was a necessary measure to protect Swiss neutrality as the recipients would undoubtedly understand. Yet the 'weight of the law' remained far from heavy and even in 1918, rarely fully imposed. Diplomatic missions felt that the lukewarm ire of their Swiss hosts was a risk worth taking when the stakes they were playing for were so high.

The Swiss themselves were implicated in an embassy scandal. What Steinberg refers to as the 'most spectacular violation of neutrality' occurred at the very top of the political hierarchy between June and July 1917 with, as Langendorff reveals, the Swiss legation in Petrograd being implicated. Councillor Arthur Hoffmann, Head of the Swiss Foreign Office, used Swiss socialist connections with the leading Bolshevik and Menshevik leaders, to act on his behalf to mediate in peace discussions between Germany and Russia. The stumbling block was that in wartime, 'Swiss neutrality forbids the conduct of an active foreign policy of any sort'. Peace between Russia and Germany would have enabled Germany to transfer troops from the Eastern to the Western Front. France, having just suffered a catastrophic defeat at the Chemin des Dames, perhaps due in part to intelligence forwarded by a spy from Geneva working for Germany in Marseille, was particularly fearful that Switzerland would allow Germany safe passage to enable the French right wing to be attacked. On this occasion, it was encrypted telegrams sent from Switzerland's 'Man in Petrograd' and decrypted by the Russians that proved to be the downfall of what became known as the 'Grimm-Hoffmann plan', as well as Hoffmann himself, who was forced to resign; a very uncommon occurrence in Swiss politics.

Whilst Hoffmann claimed that he had been acting in Switzerland's best interests, others interpreted this as acting in Germany's interests. In Steinberg's words, 'the line between what a Swiss foreign minister may or may not do is unusually delicate', and Hoffmann had overstepped the mark. Once again, the Allies felt that Switzerland was neutral in name and pro-Germany in sentiment. This was not the first time that a scandal involving encrypted telegrams rocked Switzerland and cast doubts upon the depth of the country's leaders' commitment to neutrality.

L'Affaire des Colonels

With the benefit of a century of hindsight, it seems surprising that the aforementioned warning from Chief of German Intelligence Walter Nicolaï to Bismarck that he was in danger of creating serious problems for Germany in Switzerland, did not lead to his expulsion from Bern. He was closely involved in a scandal that threatened both Swiss stability and the country's precarious neutral status. Friederich von Wattenwyl, the Swiss director of military intelligence had, in accordance with his 1909 undertaking, agreed in 1914 to share with Bismarck Swiss intelligence and (decrypted) Russian diplomatic dispatches on a daily basis. This was particularly valuable to the Germans who (according to Swiss historians, but not Barbara Tuchmann) had failed to break the Russian cypher although cryptographer André Langié, the son of a Polish refugee and a naturalised Swiss citizen from the francophone canton of Vaud, had been successfully employed by the Swiss Army to do so.

In December 1915, Langié (1871–1961) blew the whistle on Wattenwyl's activities. To Bismarck's fury, the *Gazette de Lausanne* broke the story and other francophone newspapers quickly followed. Not contained within Switzerland, the Allied press circulated the story widely. Papers as disparate as *Nelson Evening Mail* (New Zealand, 14 March 1916) and the *Hastings Standard* (England, 12 April 1916) had a field day incriminating 'Major Bismarck Military Attaché of the German Legation'. Journalists expressed confidence that 'the recall of the Military Attachés will be considered shortly'. Somewhat exonerating the role of the Swiss, they pronounced that Germany's 'diplomatic representatives are merely official spies that endeavour to corrupt the administrations and the armies in all countries where they are received'. Both papers added that the incident had caused a 'great stir' among the Swiss population. With the benefit of hindsight, historian Nicolas Gex feels that the stir was minimal, ordinary citizens unable to oppose the germanophile political élite.

Although the actions of two Swiss Army colonels, Friedrich Wattenwyl and Karl Egli, demonstrated blatant disregard for Swiss neutrality, General Ulrich Wille, himself deeply implicated, swung into action on their behalf, even telling his wife that he hoped the officers would, if needs be, 'lie their way' out of the charges. Court-martialled in February 1916, the two colonels were sentenced to a mere three weeks in prison; subsequently each was granted an honourable discharge from the Swiss Army. Sensing a real threat to Swiss neutrality and the country's standing, much of French-speaking Switzerland erupted in fury. In Lausanne, the German flag was torn down from the German consulate.

To add fuel to the flames, Wille threatened to send Swiss-German troops to Lausanne to quell the 'insurrection'. Although troops were never deployed, the threat confirmed in the Swiss-French mind that pro-Central Power leanings were 'good', or at least acceptable while pro-Entente Cordiale ones were 'bad'. At a banquet held in Lausanne in mid-April 1916, the *Gazette* reported how one of the speakers went as far as to say that he doubted whether Switzerland were truly neutral but instead was biding her time and anticipating a German victory – a victory to which both the Swiss Army (and of course a Geneva resident) might, had Wille had his way, have contributed; he had already suggested in July 1915 that Switzerland should enter the war on Germany's side. The 'Colonels Affair' was, and would remain, grist to the French mill and they were eager to use the scandal to demonstrate that the whole of Swiss Germany at least was pro-Central Powers.

A sad footnote to Langié's story is that far from receiving plaudits from the Swiss Government, he was branded a traitor. Sacked from his job, he was only able to find employment in Lausanne as a librarian. Written out of Swiss historiography of the First World War, he is not even considered worthy of mention in the *Swiss Historical Dictionary*.

If Langié had no way of defending himself – although what there was to defend is open to question – Busso von Bismarck set about damage limitation. He accused the *Gazette de Lausanne* of being more pro-French than the French newspapers themselves. He felt that the Swiss French were keen to reveal any pro-German leanings that they detected among their co-citizens. The francophone press, reviving the 'Affaire des Colonels' on frequent occasions, did little to alter his views. Nor did the newspapers [francophone at least] believe his claims that he had no agents on his pay roll and nothing to do with spies. They were right to be so dubious. In his article published post-war he admits to having helped German agents by telling them the easiest way to get out of Switzerland as well as the best attitudes to adopt when confronted by the Swiss.

What would quickly become apparent, and a point frequently reiterated by the various *Espionnage Contre-Espionnage* contributors, is that military attachés might play an important role, but the success or otherwise of agents depended very largely on how well they were handled. The 'back office' in the spy chain was crucial to an agent's continued success.

Spying a spy

In spy stories, it is the spy who takes centre stage. But a good spy is identified by a recruiter or handler and it is worth shining a light on those whose mission was indeed far more complex than simply identifying a spy, sending them to be trained, and forwarding their pay. The first step was finding someone to recruit. Small ads could yield a rich lode. Contemporary psychologist Dr Altmann notes how the German Secret Service would trawl through these ads looking for those who were down on their luck and desperate for employment. Certainly the *Gazette de Lausanne* and the *Journal de Genève* carried numerous 'Petites Annonces' in every edition. Male and female recruiters would also insert requests for commercial travellers, salesmen and shorthand typists. Such recruits were considered expendable, easy to get rid of and not worth worrying about if they were caught. Altmann believed that those recruited via this pathway were often close to being, if not already, petty criminals and accepted their mission purely out of financial necessity, a profile to which Régina, initially at least, conformed.

The famous French music-hall singer Mistinguett describes Régina's home city of Geneva as the centre of 'both German and Allied espionage' – even before hostilities were declared. She noted how the Beau Rivage Hotel – as luxurious then as it is now, was at 'the heart of international counter espionage – conspirators were noticeable everywhere.' However, only a relatively few select spies would have been entertained at, or recruited in, the Beau Rivage. For most, a park bench and a whispered conversation would have been the first step along a path that could easily lead to a lonely death in front of a firing squad.

In *Espionnage Contre-Espionnage,* Hans Fell who served with the German Intelligence Service 'in the field', claims that in certain months during 1917 (which Vuilleumier refers to as the year of 'Saturation'), there were seventy German agents working out of Switzerland (primarily in France), and only two acting on behalf of the Entente Cordiale. Like von Bismarck, he believed that any human being is 'corruptible', one just had to find their price – and pay it. However, he also admits that human emotions play a role; for some it is the appeal of danger, for some hatred, for others a desire for vengeance, and a good spymaster will tap into each would-be spy's driving force and use it to their own ends. Régina's weak points were long-standing hatred of France, what some might see as avarice, and a desire to move up in the world; there are no obvious signs of a love of danger, although Irish poet Dora Shorter believed that for many people, 'there's a joy where dangers be'.

A point little considered in spy historiography, and which Hans Fell makes, is that at the same time as spying on those whom they might entice into their web, recruiters had always to guard their own backs. While the Swiss Army (at least according to an interview with Vuilleumier and transcribed at www.liberté.ch.) was poor at catching both spies and recruiters, the Swiss Federal police, having gained experience of clamping down on the Anarchists who had fled to Switzerland primarily, but not exclusively, from Russia in the pre-war years, were more skilled. Recruiters who were caught were abandoned by their own embassy or consulates and diplomats refused to get involved, leaving them exposed to the host country's penalties. In Switzerland however, these were hardly a deterrent; on 10 December 1915 the *Journal de Genève* reported the indignation of *Schaffhauser Intelligenzblatt* at the leniency of Swiss courts towards foreign recruiters ensnaring Swiss citizens. Following the execution of Swiss citizen Niederer in Lyon on charges of spying, the newspaper expressed outrage that the German recruiter, named Sperwer, had been sentenced to a mere ten months in prison. The reluctance of their courts to impose the severe penalties that they had at their disposal was a continuous refrain in the Swiss newspapers and was in direct contrast to what was happening in France.

Fell noted that recruitment was a slow process and individuals were often observed for several weeks before being approached. Observation was a frequently complicated process, not least because the prospective spy could be a double agent, planted by the other side; several male and female spies are known to have fallen into this category. Once a potential target (spy) had either been identified or had volunteered their services, there was always the possibility (although this seems to have only happened on rare occasions) that Swiss counter-intelligence would step in, arresting both spy and recruiter on Swiss soil. A further danger, bemoaned by Fell, was that once the fully-fledged spy had been expensively trained and dispatched into France, the French authorities, tipped off by their Swiss counterparts, would pounce and the hapless spy faced lengthy imprisonment or even the death penalty – before providing Germany with any useful information. There was the added danger that the recruiter's own cover might be blown. Before 1916 the recruiter could, in such a case, be moved to another neutral country (which may have happened to Régina's initial 1910 recruiter, who disappears long before her arrest), after this date however, Entente Cordiale countries exchanged lists of suspects and circulated these to neutral states so the new host nation would be anticipating the arrival.

Having been recruited and trained, spies needed to be sent somewhere of interest to Germany where they could mingle with the local population. Fell felt that commercial travellers and those who had a legitimate reason to be out and about were particularly good at gleaning information that extended beyond the strictly military. While women would have been highly visible in militarised areas, in the civilian areas to which they were largely sent, they were almost invisible as they had 'legitimate' reasons for their peregrinations. In a port such as Marseille, shopping for food, chatting, even sitting in the sun outside a café with a soldier on leave, or walking with a convalescent from a nearby hospital, enabled them to keep a watchful eye on shipping (military and merchant) or on soldiers on leave or returning to the Front. Casual gossip or just a listening ear can reveal a wealth of information about civilian morale, of increasing interest as the war lengthened.

Principal ports were naturally sources of valuable information: which regiments were coming in, from where, which were leaving, going where, and of course the shipping itself was of significant interest. Port workers, civilians and military personnel all thronged to places of entertainment; once the ban on café-concerts and music halls had been lifted, these were ideal venues for enjoying a few leisure hours – and these places of middle/low-brow, popular entertainment needed artistes.

To German recruiters, Régina had, even before the war, appeared the ideal prospective spy, even more so when hostilities broke out. As well as having residency rights in Switzerland, as we have seen, held an Italian passport, a French-born mother, an unexplained hatred of France while her daughter, living in an orphanage in Crest, provided her with cast-iron familial reasons to travel to France. Her questionable morality, although the court did concede that her prostitution was quite 'discreet', provided ample opportunity for pillow talk. She was also an accomplished music-hall performer and, as we shall see in Chapter 8, managers encouraged performers to engage in 'friendly' relationships with clients. Her cover was watertight and she took pains to ensure that it remained so.

In wartime, women's morality frequently takes centre-stage. Showing little or no understanding of the plight of women from many walks of life whose financial situation was becoming ever harder and who resorted to spying, many of the all-male contributors to *Espionnage, Contre-Espionnage,* claim that 'the vast majority of agents are of doubtful morality [who] having wrecked their lives one way or another', are keen to act as spies. Researching trial papers, it soon becomes apparent that prosecutors would continuously refer to a woman's sexual morals. The belief that a female spy was either a whore or a vamp, or both, was widespread and a major stumbling-block for many female spies whose virtue was unquestionable but were initially unsure whether their patriotism outweighed their abhorrence for the moniker 'spy'.

While it is impossible to know the number of agents who were recruited and who, living their lives in the shadows, will remain forever in the shadows, some 120 cases of pro-German espionage were briefly reported in the *Gazette de Lausanne* and/or the *Journal de Genève* during the war. (As France frequently censored such information, the newspapers did well to report on this number of cases.) Despite the occasional intervention of the Swiss Government who might seek clemency for their own citizens (but not for those with residency rights), the majority faced the firing squad alone, their end relegated to a few lines in a newspaper at most.

Two master puppeteers were overseeing every move of spies recruited in this neutral country far from being at peace with itself. While we cannot know if either ever met Régina as they took pains to distance themselves personally from those in their web, her actions and training bear all their hallmarks; she would have been dancing to tunes that they composed both in Berlin and in Occupied Brussels.

Chapter 7

Abteilung IIIb

Say the words 'women doctors' to any Anglophone person familiar with the First World War and several names will trip off the tongue. These are the female medical practitioners and surgeons who, after significant perseverance, found ways to serve wounded and sick Allied troops. Their record is a proud one and the assistance they offered to their nations in wartime was considerable. However, it is the story of a doctor qualified not in medicine but in political sciences that has a direct bearing upon the life and death of Agent Régina Diana. This doctor's war story and that of her immediate superior, Lieutenant-Colonel Walter Nicolaï, make a significant contribution to our understanding of recruiting in Switzerland and spying in Marseille as well as to the story of Régina Diana.

Walter Nicolaï: Master Puppeteer (1873–1947)

Two years after hostilities ended, German readers with an interest in the war and the shady world of intelligence may have noticed a book by Walter Nicolaï, *Nachrichtendienst, Presse und Volkstimmung (News Service, Press and Popular Opinion)*. Despite this not making the bestseller list, there was sufficient interest for the author to follow it in 1923 with *Geheime Mächte: Internationale Spionage und ihre Bekämpfung im Weltkrieg und heute (Secret Powers: International Espionage and their fight in the World* War *and Today)*. Although neither title sounds 'snappy' to an English ear, the author was ideally placed to explore the subject for he was none other than the wartime Head of the German General Staff's intelligence service (Section 3B), *Abteilung IIIb*. Swiss historian Christophe Vuilleumieur argues that, feeling spurned by the new Weimar Republic, this ardent career soldier and monarchist was far from averse to spilling some German beans. Nor did he feel any qualms about revealing what some would have considered classified information, namely the extent to which Germany had managed to pierce both the Russian and the French Intelligence Services' wartime secrets. Whatever his reasons for publishing such sensitive material, he provides a wealth of information about the secret world of which he was master puppeteer.

The story opens in 1913 when, having cut his teeth working as a Russian analyst, gifted linguist (he spoke fluent Russian, English and Japanese), Colonel Walter Nicolaï was named Head of *Abteilung IIIb* (the principal German Military Intelligence organisation). When Nicolaï initially assumed this role, a lesser man may have been despondent. So underfunded was *IIIb* that information gathering about British and American targets had been seconded to the German Navy, leaving pre-war *IIIb* to concentrate on France and Russia. His assertion that prior to 1914 Germany's intelligence had been deprived of funds and fallen behind the perceived efficiency of the French, British and Russian organisations appears accurate. His verdict was that Germany must catch up quickly if she were not to lose the intelligence war. He immediately set about remedying the lacuna in the German operations and one of his main areas of interest was intelligence gathering by agents deep inside enemy territory.

Following his appointment, he turned his thoughts towards Switzerland and his close contact Busso von Bismarck. Very conscious of the tentacles of the French intelligence services which had established main centres in Lausanne, Basel and Geneva, he knew he would need to counter their activities and counter them fast. Irrespective of his claim that Germany had previously been too 'upright' a nation with an inherent hatred of spying, he had few qualms in seeking out men and women in neutral countries who were willing to spy for Germany. Yet, despite Nicolaï's efforts and those made by his Kriegsnachrichtenstellen (War Intelligence Bureau), Markus Pöhlmann feels that Germany never fully caught up, arguing that the 'quality of the human intelligence remained low to medium grade due [in part] to the disappointing quality of their agents' – Pöhlmann undoubtedly did not know about Régina Diana.

Be this as it may, with hostilities declared, *Abteilung IIIb's* assigned wartime tasks included information gathering in neutral or enemy countries and conducting counter-intelligence operations. It had representatives, often with consular or commercial cover, in the main neutral countries. Once Brussels fell on 20 August 1914, *IIIb* established a significant outpost at the Hotel Astoria in Brussels – a hotel which, in 1914, bristled with the highest echelons of the German Army and, most significantly of all for German Intelligence, a young woman eager to offer her services to the Fatherland. Although her biography eluded historians for decades, Walter Nicolaï came to consider her one of the very best spymasters in any intelligence service in the Great War.

Elisabeth Schragmüller An Unusual Doctor (1887–1940)

On 18 December 1919, the London *Times* carried an article 'The Blond Lady. Keeping Watch on a German Spy'. This so-called blond lady or 'Frau Doktor … spoke French without a trace of a foreign accent'. Reflecting on wartime adversaries, Vernon Kell, Head of British intelligence bureau MI5, described her as 'a woman of some ability … she inspired respect even amongst her opponents'.

Attempts to discover who this 'blond lady' was proved almost fruitless throughout the twentieth century, salacious speculation replacing hard facts. She herself assumed that the myths surrounding her were based on stories told by (a very few) German agents in France to their captors. Through these interrogations, the French intelligence service learned a grain of truth, namely that there was a bureau based in Antwerp headed by a woman whom French newspapers started to refer to as 'la sirène blonde d'Anvers', 'le tigre rouge' or 'la grande patronne' ('blonde siren of Antwerp', 'the red tiger', 'the big boss'). In his lurid 1922 text, Commandant Emile Massard provides the tantalising information that a blonde woman codenamed 'Ginger head' by the French was sometimes seen in Geneva where her chief agent was a shoemaker and cobbler named Koeninger, whose mission was to centralise information and recruit agents. Massard's information sounds accurate as he also mentions a link between Antwerp and Fribourg-en-Brisgau (since confirmed by several sources including Nicolaï). However, as Schragmüller always introduced herself to her agents as 'Mademoiselle Docteur' this would be how Régina either heard her referred to, or indeed would have known her. As Régina's father was a cobbler, this Koeninger may have been someone whom she or her lover knew.

However well known Schragmüller may have been to Walter Nicolaï and those in her employ, as Vernon Kell ruefully noted post-war, her identity was concealed; hard facts from German as opposed to French sources about this woman of many soubriquets were almost non-existent. According to Hanne Hieber, Leni Riefenstahl's proposed movie *Fraulein Doktor* never saw the light of day; in 1933 the German Defence Ministry banned spy movies. Meanwhile, the 1937 French film *Mademoiselle Docteur* and a similarly titled, equally melodramatic, British offering further muddied the waters. Even texts published at the beginning of the twenty-first century seem unable to detach themselves fully from the sensationalised accounts. However, a new generation of German and French scholars (Hanne Hieber, Chantal Anthier, Philippe Valode and Marianne Walle) have pieced together the biography of this most elusive, outstandingly gifted contributor to German intelligence, although even in 2014 in *World War One Intelligence*, Nigel West ends his entry on Elisabeth Schragmüller with the caveat 'if she ever existed'.

Recent scholarship indicates that Schragmüller's real, as opposed to fictitious, identity only came to the Allies' attention when intelligence documents fell into Russian hands at the end of the Second World War. But it was only when former Soviet archives were opened in 2000 that historians could finally supplement and corroborate the snippets. Soviet counter-intelligence's file (No. 21152) on Walter Nicolaï contained autobiographical statements, notes concerning his time as director of *Abteilung IIIb*, and correspondence between Nicolaï and Schragmüller showing that they had kept in touch at least until 1934; there was also a manuscript by Schragmüller relating to her time in the Service. Having studied the documents in considerable detail, Hieber asserts that when re-translated from Russian back to German, this MS is 'identical with an autobiographical article which first appeared in the anthology *Was wir vom Weltkrieg nicht wissen* in 1929' ('What we don't know about the World War').

The story that directly concerns the First World War and spying opens in about 1910, when a young German woman, a fluent French speaker from the Albert-Ludwig Universität in Fribourg-en-Brisgau arrived in Lausanne to spend a few months supplementing her doctoral studies. Nowadays such an arrival would pass unnoticed, but a century ago a female doctoral student from Germany would have attracted attention because Elisabeth Schragmüller was one of the first German women to enter university; this was not the pinnacle of her academic achievements however. In 1913, she completed her studies in Political Economy, defending her thesis *magna cum laude*. Styling herself Fraulein Doktor, she found employment as a social worker which brought her into contact with what she termed 'the broad strain of the population and with the working-class'. This employment, as well as the studies, was far removed from what her bourgeois family expected of their eldest daughter – her outstanding brains were considered an inconvenience for a female child. Although unbeknownst to her at the time, the job she had just begun would be short-lived nevertheless, it enhanced her knowledge and understanding of human psychology, skills she would put to excellent use in the service of her beloved Fatherland.

When war broke out, furious for not having studied medicine which might have enabled her to work with German soldiers, cursing fate that she had been born a woman and, unlike her brothers, was consequently unable to serve in the German Army, Schragmüller set off for Brussels. On her departure from Cologne in August 1914, her sister, who was performing a suitably feminine role as a nurse, reminded her to do nothing that might bring the family's reputation into ill-repute. This departure bound her fate inextricably with that of Walter Nicolaï, spies in Switzerland, and even the ill-fated Mata Hari, whom she is reputed to have recruited, trained, and finally abandoned.

Once in Brussels, showing similar determination to that of the British women whose offers of service to their country were spurned by the military authorities, she took a room in the same hotel as the newly appointed Governor General of Brussels, Wilhelm Leopold Colmar von der Golz, whom she waylaid every day requesting a job. Finally, her perseverance reaped her some reward and she was assigned to a military office dealing with security matters and from there to a bureau handling mail confiscated from Belgian soldiers. In the days before the Belgian city of Antwerp fell to the Germans, the would-be conquerors were seeking all the intelligence they could lay their hands on about troop numbers, fortifications and morale. Shragmüller's fluent French, her ability to pick out every vital nugget of information, place this in the bigger picture and provide military commanders with an accurate synthesis, brought her to Nicolaï's attention.

Deeply impressed by Schragmüller and notwithstanding her gender, Nicolaï sent her to the now German Occupied Northern French town of Lille (where British-recruited spy Louise de Bettignies would soon be operating) to undergo training, not as some rumours contend as a spy, but in military intelligence; her brains were considered too valuable to risk in the dangerous world of spying. Next she was moved to now German-held Antwerp. She was to co-lead an Intelligence Bureau, (Kriegsnachrichtenstelle). A Captain Stumpff ran the anti-British operation while she was to head up the anti-French one. Her duties included what she described in an article published in 1929 (quoted by Hieber) as the 'organisation of systematic intelligence on the large Western theatre; the recruitment of contacts [agents] and their instruction, securing the lines of communication, the de-briefing and verification of their statements and the production of reports for GHQ'. She would prove adept at all of these as well as deciding what information was reliable and what might have been sent back by agents hoping it was what the spy's handler wanted to read. She commented that she particularly enjoyed de-briefing agents and gained satisfaction when she realised that she had selected able ones.

Almost certainly unknowingly, this young German political economist was abiding by precepts advocated by the francophone, anti-Prussian Swiss military writer Baron Antoine-Henri Jomini (1779–1869), who served as a general in the French and later in the Russian armies during the Napoleonic era and has been dubbed the 'founder of modern strategy'. Unlike his archrival, German military strategist Claud von Clausewitz, Jomini recognised the value of intelligence; he stressed it was imperative for intelligence analysis to be meticulous as it was this that would enable the formation of what he termed 'reasonable and well-founded hypotheses'. Schragmüller would have agreed. She proved herself adept at forming Jomini's so-called 'hypotheses of probabilities'. Like him, she was keenly aware of the need to develop a truly workable, integrated, intelligence apparatus and also of the need to form an 'extensive system of espionage' with each spy limiting his or her reports to 'what he sees with his own eyes or hears from reliable persons'. It is interesting to note how much of Régina's intercepted information consisted precisely of what she had seen herself.

Schragmüller may have been surprised if she paused long enough to consider the part she was now playing. In an article entitled 'Mademoiselle Docteur', Marianne Walle argues that before the war, like countless other men and women of her class, this well-born university graduate saw spying as a venal undertaking which only those of questionable morality and dubious loyalty would undertake. Exposure to the real world of intelligence-gathering led her, as it would countless others, to question such misconceptions and see that to be successful, both the agencies and the agents had to form part of a highly structured, well-organised whole, where no detail should be overlooked and the better trained the agent, the more reliable their information. Their skills, not their morality, were what counted. She saw the challenge of recruiting, training and de-briefing agents as a 'mind game' to be relished and one she played to the very best of her superb intellectual abilities. She would prove a hard taskmaster, setting high standards for the spies she deployed. She soon removed those who were not up to the job. She looked upon espionage as a science which could be taught and learnt, not some sort of adventure to be undertaken for cheap thrills and a quick buck.

Shragmüller was cognisant of the types of non-military as well as military information that was required; information that could be gathered from major ports was of fundamental interest, hence the agents that she sent to these areas where, as Heibe noted, they could supply intelligence about:

> *... what human freight was shipped from the colonies, exotic countries or from America under the false flag of peaceful neutrals or the Red Cross. It was about gaining a clear picture of the dislocation of the enemy's*

> *resources in his hinterland, about the strength and the value of his reserves. It was about observing the mobilization of his new age-groups and the filling of his depots.*

Information which, to the astute or well-trained observer Régina Diana, was there for the gathering in Marseille.

Agent selection is of course the vital first step. To Schragmüller, the psychology of both those who would be recruiting for her, and those who were recruited, was important. She respected Britain's rigorous approach to recruitment but felt that France was too quick to employ those who could be 'turned' to become double agents – whom she was keen to sweep up. She was convinced that a spy must demonstrate empathy towards their sources, as co-operation provides more reliable information than coercion; she believed that women surpassed men when playing the persuading game. Nicolaï agreed with her observations. Almost certainly thanks to her brief career in social work, she also understood that a good spy could be found in unlikely places. Rather than look for academic high flyers, she was not averse to using even the barely educated. An illiterate florist in Marseille proved one of her most effective agents due to a photographic memory of which she pronounced herself to be in awe. Maybe his floristry skills extended to concealing messages via flowers placed in bouquets for café-concert artistes, messages that would find their way back to Schragmüller's desk.

Her ruthless streak was soon apparent; she quickly de-selected individuals whose aptitudes did not match her exacting standard or who did not demonstrate the required level of commitment. She appears to have had a pitiless approach to sacrificing a lesser spy to protect a more valuable one. The case of Frenchwoman Marguerite Francillard, the first female to be shot by firing squad in Paris for espionage (19 January 1917) is an example. Not a spy in the strict sense of the word, 18-year-old seamstress Francillard whose 'lover', a former Danish officer Franz de Meyerm, disguised himself as travelling silk salesman operating between France and Geneva and used her as a courier. Fraulein Doktor had a 'safe house' in Geneva where all coded messages sent and received by her agents were cleared. (Some of Régina's information would undoubtedly have been relayed to and from this address.) The messages Francillard was carrying which provided the incriminating evidence were almost certainly destined for Schragmüller who, when the young, unarguably naïve woman no longer served a useful purpose, apparently had her identified to the French Intelligence who had been watching her for some time.

Although not published in the 1936 edition of *Was wir vom Weltkrieg nicht wissen*, Schragmüller had contributed to the 1929 edition. Larger parts of her autobiographical, 'Aus dem deutschen Nachrichtendienst' were discussed and reprinted in several German newspapers (Hieber fn 74). She includes details about the difficulties in finding trustworthy agents from more privileged social backgrounds, and she compares spies along their national characteristics. She also provides information about working-class agents, travelling or commercial ones, and deserters whom she believed could contribute to espionage; she even established a Deserter Association in Geneva – under the nose of the Swiss authorities. In view of the anthology's reference to 'what we don't know', it is ironic that her true identity eluded the Allies for so long – this lack of knowledge hinders historians trying to recreate a well-rounded or balanced portrait of her.

One fascinating piece of information which Schragmüller reveals in the 1929 article is how she arranged for the close supervision of her agents' arrivals in Switzerland, be they spies or service personnel. She explained, 'the experienced agents A.F. 80, 82, 89, 90 and 91 look after travellers arriving from France with loving care. … The success is brilliant'. These 'travellers included both civilians and army personnel, including those on leave as well as deserters.' (Régina was greeted with this 'loving care' as the trial papers mention her being met at Geneva station by car despite the minimal distance between her home and the station.) Referring to her successes in summer 1916 she wrote,

> *A.F. 80 reports in detail from Geneva the statements of two colonial officers who paint a very gloomy picture of the situation and the soldiers' morale at the Somme – (Somme-offensive a bluff, breakthrough impossible)*

There may well have been an ulterior motive behind this 'loving greeting', namely to make sure that once the agent had crossed the porous Franco-Swiss border they did not fall into the Swiss authorities' hands before they had been de-briefed. Might 'A.F. 80' have been none other than Régina Diana? We know that one of her lovers was a Quarter Master on the Somme and that she also had extensive contacts with Algiers, where French colonial troops were first disembarked for the Western Front. It is tempting to surmise that he/she was.

Schragmüller acknowledged that 'loving care' included prompt and accurate payment and as money had to be spent both training and remunerating spies, she tried to ensure that Germany got good value. She would seemingly triple her best agents' salaries or give them large bonuses – although these were placed in German banks for safekeeping until after the war! Walle argues that Schragmüller realised the advantages in setting out the precise 'tariffs' for information. Remuneration was similar to that expected by artisans or the petit-bourgeois class but as the money was guaranteed, and the Germans were prompt payers, this represented a fair deal. This is borne out in trials reported in the Swiss press and also the documents relating to Régina. Schragmüller acknowledged that this honest approach bred largely honest agents; she spoke condescendingly about those who sold information to the highest bidder and those who were prepared to indulge in what she termed a 'bourse', or stock exchange of information.

Emile Massard gives details of an interview with one Constantin Condoyannis. While this text should be treated with some caution, and Massard's views on women's inefficiencies and weaknesses border on misogynistic, Condoyannis being known to be one of Shragmüller's spies makes the testimony interesting. He reported her sending his pay and the code for encrypting his correspondence via Geneva. Codes, which changed every fifteen days, were transmitted in invisible ink on wrapping paper enclosing anodyne parcels which would not have attracted the interest of either customs' officers or censors. A subsequent search of his room proved the veracity of his statement. Whether Schragmüller felt any qualms when she heard of his execution in May 1916, or indeed the execution of any other of her spies (Marguerite Francillard in January 1917 and Mata Hari in October 1917 at Vincennes) is doubtful. She may have agreed with a recruiter for the Allies in Belgium who simply told her agents, 'if you are caught it will probably be your own fault', (or, in Francillard's case, Schragmüller's own).

A School for Spies

Schragmüller would have been quick to agree that spies are formed not born, and all the main belligerents ran spy schools; the British at 8 Marine Parade, Folkestone, where Louise de Bettignies was trained, and another at Rue Soufflot, Paris. Considering German training facilities, the pre-war Chief of Austro-Hungarian Military Intelligence, Urbanski von Ostymiecz, argues that as well as being the poor relation financially, Germany's spy training was initially far less well-developed than France or Great Britain's. However, she caught up quickly.

Schragmüller oversaw 'agent academies' at Rue de la Pépinière in Antwerp (occupied Belgium), Baden-Baden and Lorräch in Germany, a few kilometres from Basel. Papers held in the Historial at Péronne indicate that the French Service de Renseignements (SR) estimated Lorräch to be the premier training centre for spies who would penetrate France from Switzerland. Both Ostymiecz and the French SR make the point that Switzerland was the 'only route' (seule voie) these spies could take to reach France.

The Fonds Vanheeckhoet (Historial Péronne) supplies useful additional information about the Lörrach centre. Recruits were interviewed, vetted, underwent training, and on successful completion of the course, charged with missions in 'enemy territory'. According to the available documents, Lörrach graduates were sent into a number of areas in France including, crucially for Régina's story, Lyon and Marseille. Frustratingly, all the index cards relating to those who were successfully trained in Lörrach were destroyed in Potsdam in 1945 which makes it impossible to know the precise number of agents and female spies Germany had operating in France. Taking as his starting point the women known to have been executed by the French, Philippe Valode estimated that these agents represent about a fifth or a quarter of the spy body; assuming that somewhere between twenty and twenty-five per cent of the agents were apprehended, he reaches a total number of some 400 agents; many, if not the majority, of whom would have entered France via Switzerland and whose Chief Controller was Fraulein Doktor Elisabeth Schragmüller.

Drawing on both British and German sources, some information is available about the curricula of spy schools. Both sides almost certainly used similar training methods and equipment. Extant material indicates long training days and courses lasted up to fourteen weeks. As well as learning to identify uniforms, regiments, and military hardware, instruction was given on topography, codes, miniature handwriting using mapping pens and Indian ink as well as the creation of and use of invisible ink – techniques with which sixteenth century Elizabeth of Bohemia and seventeenth century Aphra Behn as well as twentieth century Régina Diana were familiar. Trainees also learned how to conceal messages in accessories such as umbrellas, shoe heels, hollowed-out vegetables, and how to roll reports into tiny packages or enclose them in small pieces of rubber – rubber cut from contraceptives was popular – which could then be hidden in bicycle pumps, for example. It is worth briefly pausing over the concept of contraceptives. If pillow talk was on the agenda for female agents, and women of light virtue were intentionally recruited, then it would be in the controller's interest to supply them with condoms – a pregnant spy is of little value.

Ostymiecz lists favoured German ploys, including several used by Régina. Significant information can be sent on a postage stamp, not by writing on one but by slightly cutting the perforations; using several postage stamps on

Par ses gardiens violée,
Le chagrin l'a tuée !
(Cant. romand, verset 1er)

✝

Madame Helvétia et ses enfants Berne, Soleure, Vaud, Genève, Valais, Tessin, Fribourg, Neuchâtel, Bâle, Argovie, Zoug, Uri, Lucerne, Unterwald, St-Gall, Grisons, Thurgovie, Schaffhouse, Appenzell, Zurich, Glaris et Schwytz ;

Mesdames Constitution et Liberté ;

Leurs parentes et amies Légalité, Concorde et Egalité ;

ont la profonde douleur de faire part aux peuples du Monde civilisé du décès survenu, à Zurich, le 29 février 1916, de

Mademoiselle Neutralité Helvétia

leur chère et regrettée fille, surprise par une attaque de bocho-influenza compliquée.

Ses obsèques ont eu lieu à Berne, lundi 6 mars 1916.

Plaignons son triste sort
et gardons lui notre reconnaissance !

Saignelégier, le 7 mars 1916.

R. I. P.

Deeply ironic postcard available in Francophone Switzerland announcing the 'death' of Swiss neutrality (issued in Saignlégier, close to the Franco-Swiss border).

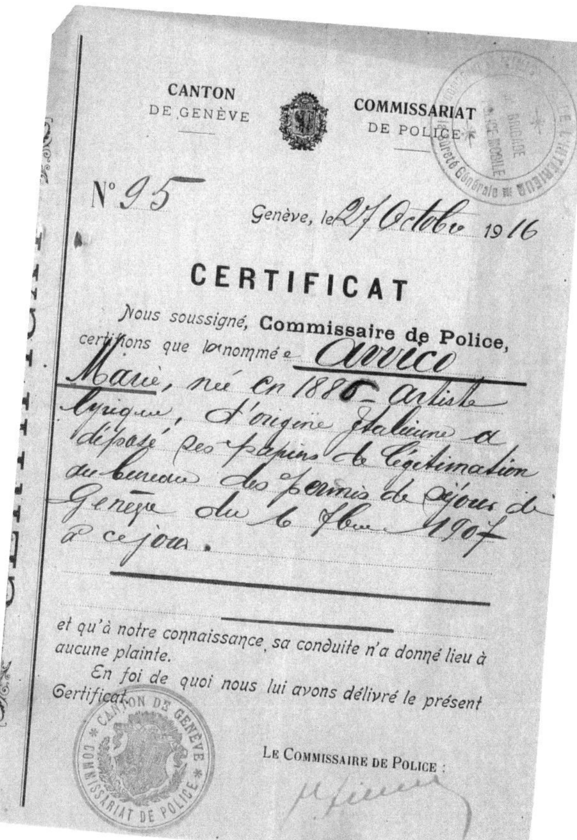

CANTON DE GENÈVE

COMMISSARIAT DE POLICE

N° 95

Genève, le 27 Octobre 1916

CERTIFICAT

Nous soussigné, **Commissaire de Police,** certifions que la nommée Arrico Marie, née en 1886 artiste lyrique, d'origine Italienne a déposé ses papiers de légitimation au bureau des permis de séjour de Genève du 6 Fbre 1907 à ce jour.

et qu'à notre connaissance, sa conduite n'a donné lieu à aucune plainte.

En foi de quoi nous lui avons délivré le présent Certificat.

LE COMMISSAIRE DE POLICE :

Foreign nationals with residency rights in Geneva were of crucial interest to German spymasters.

Passport issued by the Italian consulate in Geneva, enabling Régina to travel into France.

Geneva station in 1914 as Régina would have known it.

St Charles Station, Marseille, the departure point for overseas troops and those from the south of France moving to the Western Front, and also for spies.

Postcards such as this one of Russian troops disembarking in Marseille were freely available and do not seem to have been subject to censorship.

Postcards of 'good time girls' in Marseille were widely available; the girls were seen as a part of life in Marseille.

Main thoroughfare on which the Grand Hotel de Princes was situated.

A picture of one of Régina's soldier lovers.

Little girls were encouraged to become a 'godmother' to a soldier.

The fateful postcard with the message in invisible ink just discernible below the surface.

(Formule n° 28)

RÉPUBLIQUE FRANÇAISE

15me Région de Corps d'Armée

N° de la plainte : 262
du jugement : 770-28898

CONSEIL DE GUERRE

Dates:
du délit ...
de l'ordre d'informer ... 13 mars 1917
de la remise au rapporteur ... 13 [illegible] 1917
de la remise par le rapporteur ... 30 juillet 1917
de l'envoi à l'Etat-Major ... 14 août 1917
de la notification ... [illegible] 1917
de la séance ... 20 Septembre 1917

NOM DE L'AVOCAT

DEMANDÉ	D'OFFICE
Me J. Grisoli	

RÉSULTAT DU JUGEMENT

Mort

INVENTAIRE des pièces de la procédure suivie contre la née Avvico Marie Antoinette dite Regina Diana 31 ans se disant artiste lyrique détenue à la prison des [illegible]

inculpé de espionnage

NUMÉROS D'ORDRE	DÉSIGNATION DES PIÈCES	TÉMOINS ET RENSEIGNEMENTS
1	ordre d'informer	Dlle Ours 31-32
2 à 5	rapports de police	Talloney 33
6	note sur la Fl. Novenaz et photo jointe	Bouzid 34
7	rapport état-major	Boccaria 35
8, 9	rapport [illegible]	Commissaire divisionnaire Mr Henry 9e brigade mobile
10	procès-verbal de perquisition	
11	[illegible]	
12, 13	[illegible]	
14	audition Fl. Talloney	
15	[illegible]	
16, 17, 18	lettre [illegible] lettre Fl. Bouzid et enveloppe	
19	rapport service renseignements [illegible]	
20	[illegible]	
21, 22	lettre [illegible]	
23	[illegible]	
24 à 29	interrogatoires [illegible]	
30	audition Fl. Jouve	
31	do Dlle Ours	
33	Fl. Talloney	
34	Fl. Bouzid	
35	Boccaria	
36	Fl. [illegible]	
37	[illegible] Bergonnier	
38	[illegible]	
39	Fl. Roche	
40	Ameizon	

Certifié au nombre de cinquante [illegible] pièces plus la pièce 58 [illegible]

L'Officier d'Administration,
Greffier du Conseil,

PIÈCES DE CONVICTION

2 paquets scellés n° 532

RÉCAPITULATION

DES FRAIS A LIQUIDER EN EXÉCUTION DE L'ARTICLE 27 DU DÉCRET DU 1er SEPTEMBRE 1899

	francs
§ 1er. Transport des pièces à conviction	
§ 2 et § 3. Vacations d'experts et taxes des témoins civils	3.00
§ 4. Frais de garde des scellés	
§ 5. Indemnités aux témoins militaires	
§ 6. Port de lettres	
§ 7. Bulletin n° 1	0.40
§ 8. Prime de capture	
§ 9. Extrait du casier judiciaire	0.25
§ 10. Frais de procédure	36.00
Total des frais	39.65

AMENDES

Amende prononcée	
Décimes additionnels (en France)	
Ensemble	39.65

Audience du Vingt septembre 1917

Certifié véritable le présent relevé.

L'Officier d'Administration,
Greffier du Conseil,

Formule n° 28.

Ever bureaucratic, the cost of the trial was calculated to the last centime and charged to the deceased's estate, including witness's travel costs (3Fr) and trial costs (36Fr).

N° 15 d

MINISTÈRE
DE LA GUERRE

DIRECTION DE LA JUSTICE MILITAIRE

Bureau de la Justice Militaire

N° 01688 2/10

NOTA. — Les réponses doivent, outre le numéro d'ordre, rappeler les indications de timbre ci-dessus.

RÉPUBLIQUE FRANÇAISE

Paris, le 10 JAN 1918

LE SOUS-SECRETAIRE D'ETAT DE LA JUSTICE MILITAIRE
à Monsieur le Général Commandant la 15e région
MARSEILLE.

Je vous confirme les termes de mon télégramme du 4 janvier 1918, N° 484-2/10, répondant à votre transmission du 11 novembre 1917.

M. le Président de la République n'a pas cru devoir accueillir le recours en grâce présenté à l'égard de la nommée AWICO (Marie-Antoinette), dite Regina Diana que le conseil de guerre de la 15e région a condamnée le 20 septembre 1917, à la peine de mort pour espionnage et tentative d'espionnage.

Je vous prie de vouloir bien donner toutes instructions utiles pour que la sentence soit exécutée dans le plus bref délai possible, et m'adresser un duplicata du procès-verbal établi pour la constater.

Je vous renvoie ci-joint le dossier de la procédure.

Pour le Sous-Secrétaire d'Etat et par son ordre,
Le Directeur-adjoint de la Justice Militaire,

15e RÉGION
Etat-M...
Bureau de la Justice Militaire
N° 1345

Transmis à M. le Commissaire du Gouvernement près le Conseil de guerre ... Marseille

12 Janv. 18

15e RÉGION — LE GÉNÉRAL COMM...

15e ... Armée
Date d'Ar...
11 JANV ...
883
N° au réperto...
Remis au ...

No hope of reprieve. The letter confirming French President Poincaré had rejected the plea for clemency.

The Marseille firing range where Régina and other spies were executed.

Marie-Antoinette's death certificate, with nothing to suggest that this was an unusual death.

ÉTAT-CIVIL

REG. 3

N° 10

Le présent ne peut, en aucun cas, être considéré comme acte légal.

MAIRIE DE MARSEILLE

L'Acte de Décès de Marie Antoinette Avrico - fille de Joseph - décédée le cinq janvier 1918

a été inscrit le 7 dit dans les Registres de l'Etat-Civil de cette Ville.

Délivré pour note, à la Mairie, le 19 janvier 1918

LE CHEF DU BUREAU DE L'ÉTAT CIVIL,

IMP. MOULLOT - MARSEILLE - 1866 - Type 5

a letter increased the amount of information being relayed – a useful strategy as Swiss censorship of letters became ever more assiduous. German-trained spies learnt to conceal messages in inflammable tubes in cigars or cigarettes which could be lit if the spy were approached. One cannot help but wonder if the cigarette Régina is holding to her lips in one photograph conceals information vital to her spymasters. Undoubtedly she would have received bouquets at the end of some of her music-hall acts. Did these contain hidden messages? Both Roegels and Ostrymiecz, note how recipients of bouquets could find messages amidst their blooms, while flowers worn decoratively with their stems or leaves bent in a particular way could be used to pass on information. Régina's files contain multiple pictures, letters with stamps, photographs and postcards; all assume new significance when seen with a spycatcher's eye.

The Power of the Post

Once information has been gathered, its relevance is short-lived and it must be sent back quickly. Working on Germany's behalf in Paris, Agent S796 (no further information has been found, although almost certainly one of Schragmüller's stable), would write a report using invisible ink, send it to Geneva where it arrived the next day. Having been dropped into a safe 'letter box', a courier would pick it up and it would be read in Germany twenty-four hours later.

'Letter boxes' were at the heart of effective spy operations. Initially, letters were addressed Poste Restante and would simply be retrieved from the local post office. However, all belligerents soon clamped down on letters sent Poste Restante and local post offices also became suspicious. As the French postal authorities had, according to Hans Fell, compiled a list of pro-German businesses in Switzerland, and would have monitored communications to these premises, a personal address was preferable; Régina used her home address, Rue de Fribourg in Geneva, and two 'pensions' in Zurich.

Another simple ruse also used by Régina was one connected with letters. Switzerland was famous for its hotels; some of which had fallen on hard times. Address a letter to a fictitious hotel resident, the hotel porter who deals with the post would simply put it to one side and either waited for it to be collected or forwarded it on to another address, often in a town like Zurich. The most trusted porters might even forward letters to Germany – or indeed any other destination as post from Switzerland could travel the world, unlike letters sent from belligerent countries, many of which were of course totally innocent. Not every envelope concealed information valuable to the enemy.

According to Fell, for those wishing to send and receive less innocent letters, recruiting letter box 'keepers' was straightforward. Placed at little risk, these individuals were suitably remunerated for their pains. Almost all recruiters stress that recruiting for all forms of espionage work – which stretches far beyond spying in foreign territory, is easy among those who are facing financial disaster and thanks in part to Schragmüller, Germany was a generous and speedy paymaster.

Eventually, aware of the abuse of the postal system through the actions of spies, the Swiss Federal Government informed the Post Office that it no longer needed to respect the code of confidentiality that lies at the heart of the postal system; letters were routinely opened and censored. This was another of the liberties which, to the outrage of many Swiss citizens (including a Swiss Army lawyer), was lost during the war and over which discontent rumbled until November 1918 (*Journal de Genève* 2 July 1916; 31January 1917). Despite ordinary Swiss correspondents paying the price for the illegal actions of spies and handlers planted in their midst and (ab)using their territory, the authorities were nevertheless justified in taking such actions; there is ample evidence that agents working for all sides were sending information through the Swiss postal system. To cite just two examples, Régina's trial documentation shows coded letters exchanged with Switzerland, whilst Luxembourgeoise Lise Rischard sent copious information from Lausanne to her British handlers in Paris and England. Morgan reveals how one letter contained multiple inaccuracies about the Lausanne region which should have alerted a censor that a code was being used, albeit unskilfully, yet the letter continued its journey undetected. At times, censors were undoubtedly slack.

'Beyond the reach of ordinary men'

We will never know if Walter Nicolaï or Elisabeth Schragmüller ever read Chinese general, military strategist, and philosopher Sun Tzu's fifth century BC classic text *The Art of War*. Considering spies, he noted that:

> *What enables the wise sovereign and the good general to strike and conquer, and achieve things beyond the reach of ordinary men, is foreknowledge.*

Familiar with Sun Tzu or not, the war service of both Walter Nicolaï and his right-hand woman Dr Elisabeth Schragmüller, demonstrates that not only were they intellectually aware of the 'good general's' need for foreknowledge, they did everything in their power to glean it. Using their skills, aptitudes and understanding of both the craft of spying and the psychology of the undercover agent, they ensured that their Fatherland was provided with the best information they could buy about the enemy: his troops, shipping, military dispositions and his morale. They kept this flowing until the last shot had been fired and they had finally, albeit reluctantly, to accept that all their efforts had not brought the victory that they had worked so hard and so ruthlessly to deliver.

Chapter 8

To Victory We Sing

On Friday 13 November 2015, an attack at the Bataclan Concert Hall in Paris killed ninety predominantly young men and women, forty more lost their lives in other Parisian venues and some 200 were injured. The following Tuesday 71,233 fans from England, France and across the world, travelled to London's Wembley Stadium to watch a 'Friendly' football match between France and England. Far more important than the outcome of the match was the demonstration of solidarity with a country in mourning. As the notes of the French national anthem, *La Marseillaise,* filled the winter sky, dignitaries from both countries, football players, spectators and fans, united in song. For some, it was the first time they had ever sung in French, maybe they didn't fully understand the words, but the emotion as thousands of voices filled the air was palpable. Somehow, getting the words quite right or even pronouncing them correctly was unimportant. What was important was that the whole crowd was singing its defiance against acts of terrorism.

Almost exactly 101 years ago, at the self-same Bataclan and other places of popular entertainment across France, soldiers and civilians had also joined together in song, for France already had a long tradition of 'political' singing in streets, café-concerts and music halls. Although the government had closed these places of popular entertainment as soon as war was declared, bowing under public pressure in late November 1914, the authorities accepted that they should be re-opened. The French and their army of music-hall artistes and performers would now, as one song put it, *Sing our way to Victory*. But in reality, it was not only patriotic French singers who would be leading the nation in song.

Patriotic Songs for Loyal Citizens

Over the past few decades Anglo and francophone historians have explored the role and importance of song, café-concert and music hall in French popular culture and even in pedagogy. Their work helps us to understand the public face of the person whom newspapers referred to slightly incorrectly as 'the pretty Swiss singer, Régina Diane'.

Laura Mason argues that if in Ancien Régime or pre-revolutionary France, street singers or *chansonniers* had been considered tawdry and not even on the fringes of decent society, this changed with the French Revolution; its seismic shifts in French society also made their mark on street music. Popular singing of revolutionary songs was constructed as a patriotic duty which combined what Mason refers to as both 'notions of community and support of the revolutionary cause'. Between 1793 and 1794, singing suddenly became 'politically correct', henceforward, citizens of the new Republic would, in the translated opening words of *Le Chant du Départ* 'achieve Victory by singing [La Victoire en chantant]'. These songs expressed notions of community and revolutionary ideals, ideals which could be adapted to suit the purposes of changing political times.

If the French Revolution created the most fundamental social upheaval in France, the greatest emotional one was the War of 1870. Songs written in the previous seven decades had captured, commented on, and satirised political events; now a new theme entered musicology: *Revanchist* or 'Revenge'. Countless songs lamented the loss of the provinces of Alsace and Lorraine, determination to seek vengeance and return these 'daughters' to France's bosom. But this would require a further clash with Germany and martial, patriotic words such as those of '*Alsace et Lorraine*' and '*Le Regiment de Sambre et Meuse*' heralded the forthcoming struggle. (So important did this latter song become in the 1914–1918 psyche that it was played as those condemned for treasonable activities against France, including spying, were led to the execution post.) Songs anticipating a future, albeit 'just', war against Germany were sung across France, even becoming a powerful weapon in mobilising electoral support during the ensuing, politically troubled years 1871–1914. Cultural historian Glenn Watkins argues that the war of 1914 was prepared for as much in the café-concerts as by the General Staff.

During the early decades of the French Third Republic (1870–1940), the French educational system underwent significant changes. As early as 1872, the Minister for Public Instruction initiated pupils' introduction to 'proper' songs; songbooks and singing lessons were to form part of the curriculum from a very young age. Like the teaching of poetry in England in the late nineteenth century, the teaching of songs was seen to hold multiple benefits: literacy, memory skills and, through carefully selected songs, an understanding of the nation's culture and the child's proper place therein. By singing outside, pupils could even benefit from a good dose of fresh air while expanding their lungs! By the 1880s and early 1890s, young, impressionable citizens belted out songs that proclaimed love of 'la Patrie', the sacred duty to regain Alsace Lorraine and aspirations of 'triumph and our glory' – if these actions were performed in a legitimate call to arms and defensive action. Although unforeseen by the early pedagogues who were so keen to introduce singing, this was the generation that would sing its way to the Front, be celebrated in the lyrics performed by the predominantly female artistes in café-concerts and music halls who encouraged audiences to pour adulation on the heroes of this 'just' war, and included France's Allies in their paeans of praise.

Not all songs portrayed the whole nation in a positive light however. Arch-patriot, politician and founder of the Ligue des Patriotes, Paul Déroulède's hugely popular pre-war *Chants du soldat* (Soldiers' Songs) lauded the perceived courage of France's soldiers – but one geographical area was excluded from praise. His song *De Profundis* was scathingly uncomplimentary about 'lui de Marseille' (him from Marseille) who, lacking patriotic sentiments, preferred to be a bystander, saving his own skin and watching his comrades die rather than sacrifice himself, 'Dans tous les duels, il faut des témoins/Nous serons les témoins des Français de France'. (Every duel needs witnesses/We'll be the witnesses of France for the French.) Composed in the early 1870s, still sung in the immediate run-up to the First World War, this song would have a profound effect on soldiers from Marseille three decades later.

Control over, or censorship of, songs and indeed all spoken and printed media was part of cultural life long before that shot rang out at Sarajevo; French censors already exercised iron control over both songs and the venues in which they were sung. According to historian Régina Sweeney, even in the 1870s, cultural censors started from the premise that 'everything was suspect', if not politically then at least morally, and when hostilities opened, they were on the 'prowl' not only for possible divulgence of information that would be militarily useful to the enemy but, just as importantly, words or lines that could endanger either public morale, morals or both. The well-oiled French bureaucratic process was ready to swing into immediate action. Perhaps anticipating more militarily serious matters to pre-occupy him, the Military Governor of Paris handed over control of songs, both lyrics and tunes, to the Parisian Prefect of Police (Emile Laurent, appointed 2 September 1914) whose business the censorship of some 16,000 songs would henceforth become. Irrespective of the public space in which it was sung, every song would be scrutinised by an army of censors – their precise number lost to history, although we know that a former Police Commissioner, one Monsieur Martin, was particularly assiduous in his duties. Sweeney argues that the French government was alone among the belligerent powers in censoring songs in this centralised manner thereby underlining the recognised place of song in French political life. They appear to have been less adept at controlling the loyalty of the singer to France's cause.

Monsieur Martin and his battalion of undoubtedly middle-class and predominantly, if not exclusively, male colleagues, enthusiastically sharpened their blue pencils and they remained sharp. As the French press had been censored for some thirty years, the wartime censorship of songs which lasted from August 1914 to October 1919 would prove unchallenging to these experienced bureaucrats. If the primary censor was unsure as to a song's suitability, he could refer it up to the comforting omniscience of the Parisian Police Prefect. Should censors be growing concerned about their contribution to the war effort, in 1916 they were reassured by government minister Aristide Briand that, 'the moral behaviour of the country is as important as cannons and guns'; 'moral behaviour' extended to places of popular entertainment. Such attitudes about morality and the minister's concerns played conveniently into the hands of the bourgeoisie, who had long expressed dismay at working-class 'immorality'

Extensive records in the Paris Préfecture de Police relate to censorship of songs and control over how these were performed as well as documenting attempts by composers to have negative decisions reversed. Several French cultural historians have traced the life of songs in impressive detail. Awareness of these controls allow us to understand the types of songs which Régina would have sung in Marseille (where Paris led, the provinces followed) and even how she had sung them as every gesture had to conform to what had been approved when the song was granted that all important visa. Obtaining a visa was far from a simple rubber stamp exercise. Songs had to promote the war effort but not comment upon its conduct. We can be sure that although at least some of the songs Régina sang were written by Swiss lyricists, they would have been cleared by either the Parisian or Marseille prefecture, the latter led by Abraham Schramel.

French song archives hold countless examples of 'non visée' songs, sometimes with illuminating commentary. A visa could be withheld because a sentence was deemed 'unsuitable', at others times because a verse or theme was considered offensive or detrimental to the war effort. Occasionally, censors also seem to have taken upon themselves to be guardians not only of French morale and morals, but of the French language itself. Anne Simon-Carrère juxtaposes two songs, one which was turned down largely due to the censor considering that the French language would be none-the-poorer for its suppression(!) and the other because, by highlighting a mother's painful thoughts about her son's departure for the Front, it could lower morale. Some outraged songwriters went to considerable lengths to adapt their pieces to gain the necessary visa.

Even the tunes were subject to the censor's eagle ear. The sacred sounds of *La Marseillaise, La Brabançonne* (Belgium's national anthem) and, one imagines, *God Save the King*, could not be tampered with, although the Russian national anthem appears to have been less sacrosanct. There was also a ban on the use of proper names for fear one or more of these might 'coincidentally' bring a leader into disrepute, although songs about 'Rosalie' – the poilus' name for the bayonet – proliferated; later in the war 'Rosalie' lewdly morphed into Rose-à-lit [Rose-in-bed]. However, as soldiers were being given leave in order to repopulate the nation, perhaps this was acceptable. Simon-Carrère reveals that leave came to be known as *spermissions*, although I have found no reference to this ribald soldier slang in song. Songs hinting at adultery were banned as these could lower the morale of those whose precious six days' leave (including travelling time) was coming to an end, or indeed convalescents far from home who were frequently entertained at café-concerts. By contrast the song that affirmed a young fiancée's determination to remain faithful to her wounded and disfigured hero met with great approval – by the censors at least – and featured widely in café-concert programmes.

Neutral states could not be satirised or even gently mocked in any way for fear or putting pressure on potential allies or even, however implausible this may seem, throwing them into the arms of the enemy. At least until the summer of 1917 and the very significant unrest in the French Army, trench songs or those sung near the Front Line were not subject to such rigorous controls; there is evidence of soldiers' songs berating *les neutres*, with the Swiss coming in for opprobrium. Had the home front known about this poilus' song, Geneva-born Régina with her lusty rendition of a Swiss-composed song *Salut aux Alliés (Hail to the Allies)* may have provided some antidote. Surely she was helping the French sing their way to Victory.

Obtaining a song's necessary visa was but half the battle. Long before the war, officials frequently distrusted public gatherings and performances particularly in establishments favoured by the poorer classes. Police or gendarme officers would attend dress rehearsals to evaluate costumes, sets and gestures, and even when a performance had been 'cleared', police informers entered the various places of entertainment, mingled with the crowds and reported back on the songs being sung; if these did not accord word for word with the version that had been visée, the song and even the whole act would be pulled. These unannounced visits revealed both how the song was delivered and its effect on the audience, not to mention the singer's interpretation. Not even a singer's arched eyebrow escaped this draconian surveillance. How many singer-spies were themselves being spied upon by the gendarme-spies?

With such controls in place and with the police exercising ruthless power over popular entertainment, performers and performance venues had little choice than to appear one hundred per cent behind the war effort; loyalty had to be both fixed and transparent. If this were in any way in question, closure or withdrawal of the programme and substantial financial loss followed. Few owners or performers would have been unaware that the French government had, as we shall see, significant experience of closing places of both popular and highbrow entertainment. As Sweeney notes, the authorities had long watched for seeds of discontent or moral corruption to grow in the fertile spaces of the café-concerts.

A Very Gallic Knees-Up

If the French were going to sing their way through the war, albeit only through the expression of appropriate, carefully regulated sentiments, the ideal venue, the café-concert, had been integral to popular culture for almost two centuries. The origins of the first café-concert, known as *café chantant*, reach back to 1731; their popularity increased exponentially during the Revolution. By the middle of the nineteenth century, these were burgeoning in cities large and small.

During the Second Empire (1852–1870) when industrialisation saw an exodus, initially of men and subsequently families, from the countryside to the towns; the café-concerts flourished. By the 1860s, they ranged from what Kelley Conway terms 'dives' (*bouis-bouis*) to 'sumptuous palaces clustered along the Champs-Elysees and the grands boulevards of the Right Bank' – the Bataclan, where this chapter started, threw open its doors for the first time in 1864. The largest venues could accommodate over 2,000 customers in the main 'salle' and frequently included a billiard room and a large garden to supplement the main concert area. By 1894, Paris had as many café-concerts as theatres and the most successful of them, L'Olympia, grossed 2 million francs – more than the famous theatre La Comédie-Française. Cultural historian Pierre Echinard has calculated that by 1900 there were over 300 café-concerts in Paris alone and although there were fewer per capita in the provinces, there was no lack of choice for clients, particularly in cities such as Marseille. Even the provincial café-concert names echoed those of the capital.

Yet, like all other places of entertainment in Belle-Époque France, café-concerts and music halls did not flourish unrestricted and unsupervised. From the mid-1860s up until 1906 when the rules were briefly relaxed only to be re-introduced with a vengeance in 1914, all places of public entertainment were subject to tight police control. Every morning, armed with a copy of the evening's proposed entertainment, directors had to report to the Prefect of the Police to have their programme approved. Proprietors appear to have considered these controls and police intrusion an acceptable inconvenience largely due to the café-concerts' popularity with all classes and hence their financial viability. Sweeney argues that it was this experience which enabled café-concert and other proprietors to cope with the wartime censorship bureaucracy so easily and allowed censorship to be so quickly mobilised.

Despite the plethora of controls, numerous venues trod a thin line between being places of popular entertainment and *maisons closes* (brothels) where singers were expected by the end of the performance to have enticed patrons to prolong their evening's entertainment. Some directors even went so far, at least if Régina's contemporary, the renowned music-hall star and spy Mistinguett is to be believed, on insisting on 'director's bedding rights' which she terms 'droit de cuissage'.

As prostitution became increasingly regulated in nineteenth century France, opening a café-concert provided a convenient loophole. Notwithstanding the ability of prefectures to control the words that were sung and the acts that were performed, they were less adept at controlling public behaviour, although rules stressed the need for morality ('bonnes moeurs') amongst public and artistes alike. There is little firm evidence from contemporary writers that these were strictly adhered to – and strong indications that they were not.

Not all café-concerts were overtly sleazy. At some, frequented largely by the 'respectable' working and lower-middle classes, the working man and his wife or sweetheart could, according to the 1902 popular song *Viens Poupoule*, enjoy for the price of a cup of coffee, (20 centimes in Paris, less in the provinces) hours of entertainment performed by more or less accomplished singers. In a similar manner to silent movies, a billboard announcing, 'Re-order now' was paraded when acts changed over. As for the type of songs Poupoule and her companion heard, Charles Rearick reveals these predominantly 'highlight[ed] the pains and deaths of a good little people'. Café-concert proprietors and directors were quick to enumerate their establishments' multiple benefits; the informal atmosphere was such that the worker in his overalls, the toff in his top hat and the little woman in her best shawl, felt equally welcome. They could rub shoulders with each other and, an advantage for the single man at least, meet what were euphemistically called 'femmes publiques' (public women) whose presence became of ever-increasing concern from 1916.

The ambiance in both respectable and less respectable café-concerts was both boisterous and asphyxiating, drink flowed freely, smoking was ubiquitous, gas lighting was used (electricity was introduced in the better class establishments in the 1890s) and customers circulated as and when they pleased, calling out and interacting with performers, joining in the refrains and singing-along to the well-known songs they had learned at school; when they had had enough, they simply got up and left. Looking at her physiognomy, (one of her lovers told the military tribunal that he appreciated her 'corpulence énorme'), Régina appears to have had a pair of powerful lungs, a prerequisite for café-concert artistes, whose voices had to be audible above the cacophony of sounds. Turning to the proprietors of café-concerts, overheads were gratifyingly low; each 'tour de chant' (singing turn) involved only one singer who provided his or her own music and was expected to perform more than fifty songs in an evening. To make sure that café-concerts did not compete with traditional theatre, every word had to be sung; spoken words were prohibited, rendering gestures important – as she would prove in captivity, although this time to her detriment, Régina excelled at these. Wigs, dancing, and pantomime, indeed anything that competed with mainstream theatre, was prohibited. When café-concerts and music halls reopened their doors in November 1914, they had moved much closer together, controls had been significantly relaxed and the fine line between the two forms of entertainment was increasingly blurred: songs could now be interspersed with theatrical-style performances by stereotypical buffoons.

Marseille had a well-established tradition of café-concert and music hall by the time Régina, already an experienced performer, arrived. Its largest venue, the Alcazar, decorated to look like the Alhambra in Grenada (it survived in various guises until the 1970s), could seat 2,000 patrons. With its huge organ, orchestra of thirty-five musicians, galleries and private boxes, it was France's largest café-concert. Echinard points out the clientèle also comprised significant numbers of dockworkers and sailors, some proved prime for Régina's picking and providers of essential information. In 1911,

Marseille had a population of over 555,000; during the war, the departing foreigners were replaced by casual dockworkers, Northern French, Belgian and Serbian refugees, patients and convalescents from Marseille's seventeen hospitals and, from July 1915 when leave was finally instituted, large numbers of soldiers (including ones from France's overseas colonies) on leave, known as 'permissionnaires'. Régina would have had no difficulty in gaining employment in one of Marseille's many places of entertainment where patriotic works with suitably stirring titles such as 'Patrie!' were constantly performed. By fraternising with soldiers, sailors or dockworkers, some of whom proved willing to share snippets of information and seemingly harmless gossip with a friendly artiste, Régina was merely fulfilling the terms of her unwritten contract to the café-concert proprietor and, more sinisterly, to her spymasters. As Fräulein Doktor [Elisabeth Schragmüller] knew so well and would inculcate into her spies, snippets pieced together build up a powerful picture. The well-trained spy will be attentive to even seemingly casual remarks and forward these on to their handler. With artistes being expected to mingle with clients, a café-concert was the perfect cover for a singer spy.

Geneva too had followed the café-concert trend. In the 1880s the Brasserie de L'Espérance had opened its doors at 42 Rue de Carouge. Situated in a bustling area of the city, it was one of many venues offering similar entertainment to that available in France. Its owners' multiple requests for permission to extend the premises, not to mention the significant amounts of money they invested, are testimony to its success. Joël Aguet has painstakingly traced the architectural and planning permission developments and concludes that such venues were important in Geneva's cultural life. If L'Espérance were at the higher end of the café-concert market, a letter of 8 June 1917, pertaining to Régina, submitted to the French courts and signed by M. Monnet in Geneva, confirms that Geneva harboured many (not always salubrious) venues where artistes could hope for little more than modest takings, many being forced, like Régina, to supplement their earnings in other ways – including prostitution.

Léon Labarre's dramatic fantasy set in a Geneva café-concert demonstrates that these venues remained well frequented in wartime Geneva, welcoming the same cross-section of humanity as could be found across the border in France. Although there would have been inevitably far fewer *permissionnaires* than in French cities, French soldiers on leave in places such as Annemasse, as well as the deserters who had flocked to Switzerland, would inevitably have formed part of the clientèle on any given evening. Experience in Geneva's café-concert would be invaluable in a spy who could subsequently be moved across the border. For Régina, honing newly-acquired spying and longer-standing singing skills in her city of residence would have been a natural undertaking – and spy stories reported in the francophone Swiss press frequently mention 'singers' being plum targets for recruiters.

However plush and opulent or sleazy and run-down the venue, long before as well as during the war, the life of a café-concert artiste, irrespective of her virtue, was the dark underbelly of these seemingly light-hearted places of popular entertainment. All who worked there, but especially women, faced a precarious and harsh existence. Café-concerts' glitzy public spaces did not extend behind the scenes. More than one eye-witness attests to the changing-rooms where they stored the outfits they had to provide for themselves being filthy, tobacco fumes from hundreds of smokers almost asphyxiated them, and the gas jets of the performance areas were turned high enough to, as one artiste put it, 'roast' them. Proprietors took a large cut from any proffered tips, contracts were exploitative with singers expected to be constantly available – and not only for performances and rehearsals. A repertoire of dozens of songs was required – the programme changed fortnightly, and the artiste had to be able to lead the audience in singing in parts of the programme as well as belt out her own solo songs in a voice loud enough to drown out the more raucous sections of the spectators.

Apart from artistes with an established reputation, both genuine singers and those who used singing as a cover for prostitution (or spying) were often, as Dominque Delord points out, forced to take lodgings as directed by the proprietor; rents and meals were often exorbitant and, with no fixed salary, life was precarious. Although attempts were made to regulate these practices, there is no indication that even as late as 1906 this was successful. When the café-concerts were finally re-opened in late 1914, the government of a country at war would have felt it had more important concerns than the exploitation of working-class women in areas of popular and lowbrow entertainment even those who were, outwardly at least, patriotically keeping up both home front and poilu morale.

Music hall artiste Mistinguett, who by 1914 had a well-established career in music hall which lasted many decades, provides insights into the seamier side of life for those who did not enjoy her level of success. 'If the house were won over, they sang along, if not they bombarded unfortunate players with cherry pits and orange peel.' Mistinguett and Régina's contemporary, Yvette Guilbert, conjures up an image full of pathos. Having observed a performance in Lyon she noted:

> *Perspiring, panting, her fat body heaving with excitement, her arms red with the heat, she looked like some great lobster… Never for the life of me have I been able to recall her name but I shall not easily forget the infinite sadness that descended on my soul at the sight of her. I was aghast.*

If the rewards were considerable for those who made it to the top of the profession, for the less talented or less lucky, the opportunity to supplement scant resources by spying would have been tempting. Easy pickings for recruiters, some may have hoped to accumulate sufficient funds to enable them to leave such a poisonous atmosphere behind them; others would have already been facing very significant financial hardship for in the war's opening months, it had looked likely that café-concerts would remain closed 'for the Duration.'

Almost unable to 'Sing our way to Victory'

Many British people who have tried to deal with smaller French businesses during the summer months will be aware of the frustrations of trying to get work done or orders processed during August. Still today, this is the sacred holiday month when much of provincial France seems to shut down and it is most definitely not 'Business as Usual'.

When war broke out in August 1914, theatres in Paris were closed, as was traditional for the month. The authorities were determined that they and indeed all places of public entertainment would remain so, even cafés were expected to be closed by 10pm. To slightly misquote poet Rudyard Kipling, with the Hun almost 'at [Paris's] gate', the nation at war was to be a serious nation. Initially this was not too significant a problem because many Parisians, remembering the Siege of 1870 had, like the Government, fled southwest to the Bordeaux area. Some male actors and performers such as music hall star Maurice Chevalier (who had made his debut in Marseille) had rushed to re-join their regiments whilst others removed themselves from France's troubled shores by going to neutral countries such as Switzerland or even America. A state of siege had been pronounced and with the Battle of the Marne fought so close to the capital, the remaining Parisians' thoughts would not have immediately turned to the theatre; citizens in distant Marseille had, as we shall see in Chapter 9, more pressing concerns than theatres and concert halls. With 27,000 French soldiers killed on August 22nd 1914 at Charleroi, the mood was truly sombre.

By October 1914 the immediate threat to Paris had lifted (although the government remained in exile until 22 December), and Parisians began drifting back, some seemingly embarrassed by their lack of resilience. They returned to a silent city, café-concerts, music halls and theatres were firmly shut, and appeals to the Paris Police Prefect to reverse the decision fell on deaf ears. It would, it was claimed, give the wrong impression to the fighting man if those at home were enjoying themselves while he and his comrades were engaged in a struggle of such epic proportions that by December 1914 France had lost 400,000 men.

If civilian places of entertainment were silenced, the same was not true of the hospitals. Eugénie Buffet, an internationally renowned artiste of the café-concert scene was, like many of her compatriots, nursing with the Red Cross. She soon noticed that singing the familiar songs they had learned in the schoolroom transported the wounded back to the carefree world of home and childhood. These songs even soothed moribund soldiers; singing sometimes eased them into the next life. She gives a moving account of the sense of peace that descended upon horrifically wounded men when she raised her voice in the well-known songs of home. She decided that rather than nurse, her war work would be to sing for France's wounded heroes and the small ambulant troupe she quickly formed travelled around hospitals and convalescent areas in the Paris region. As with British troops, increasing numbers of French performers, some, like Buffet, already 'big names', gave concerts for both the wounded and those on rotation out of the line.

Non-combatants tried to creep in to the concerts which Buffet was giving for wounded and convalescent poilus – the only groups for whom entertainment was not considered inappropriate. Aware of civilians' eagerness to hear and even join in the singing, she reached a pragmatic decision. A small number could attend if they contributed to the entertainment either by making monetary donations or distributing song sheets, tobacco or other small comforts, their presence at the *spectacles* thereby being constructed as patriotic. There is evidence of such concerts being provided in hospitals in Marseille as well as in the open-air spaces of La Calèche. Singers with a more sinister agenda than providing morale-boosting songs could have passed undetected. Hospital statistics and reports on the morale of the wounded would be part of the 'chatter' that skilled spymasters such as Schragmüller would feed into the bigger picture being forwarded to Berlin.

Another group of war workers who were, in England at least, entertained by concerts were munitions workers. Singers and vaudeville artistes came into the factories and provided free entertainment during precious 30-minute lunch break. The information that an observant entertainer could glean about the factory, its output and workers' morale would have been of great interest to any spymaster. As Nicholas Hiley pints out, the Ministry of Munitions went so far as to develop its own spy department, P.M.S.2. If this were also the case in France, Schragmüller and other handlers would have been keen to encourage their singer/agents to penetrate into the munitions factories, of which there were several in Marseille. In these, as in most French factories, industrial relations became increasingly acrimonious as the war lengthened.

If poilus (and munitions workers) were being entertained or aided towards convalescence in these early months, for most civilians, café-concerts, music halls and theatres remained firmly locked. However, by 13 September, the Germans had been turned away from Paris. Surely, the lobbyists claimed, it was time for *la vie normale* to be gradually extended to places of entertainment. Opponents argued, equally passionately, that with parts of Northern France in German hands, French troops being slaughtered, Alsace and Lorraine still not reunited with France, hundreds of families in mourning and thousands enduring the pain of separation, frivolity as represented in café-concerts, music halls and theatre was unacceptable. The Prefect of Paris agreed with the anti-brigade and his word filtered down to the other metropolitan areas. The Marseille newspaper *Le Sémaphore* applauded the decision on 3 September, for this was the time 'neither for rejoicing nor amusement' ('L'heure n'est pas aux réjouissances ni aux amusements').

Would-be spectators and theatre managers continued to clamour loudly but unsuccessfully for a lifting of the ban which, beyond people's desire for a few hours' entertainment, or even oblivion, was having one very serious consequence. Before the war, there had been 75,000 men and women whose livelihood depended on the entertainment industry. Some were naturally of military service age and consequently found themselves at the Front. However, a significant number were not. By November 1914, according to one newspaper, 20,000 people whose livelihood depended upon popular entertainment in Paris alone were totally deprived of financial means and were even resorting to the free meals being distributed in the Jardin de Paris or the Eldorado. They were thus a drain upon the public purse. Marseille theatre directors mustered the same argument and the Marseille Cinéma des Variétés jumped the gun, re-opening on 23 October 1914 with a British film entitled *Called to the Front*. The Paris Opéra-Comique manager who was now assisting General Gallieni (Military Governor of Paris) added his voice to that of the pro-entertainment lobbyists. Perhaps his suggestion that these ever-popular venues would boost civilian morale, and thereby the war effort, held sway. A cheerful population emerging from an evening spent in patriotic song or watching suitably uplifting plays, including ones depicting valiant poilus, would prove that despite numerical superiority, the Boches could not diminish French steadfastness. Parisian venues lead the way, albeit with restricted opening days and hours, and those in the provinces rapidly followed. Throughout the war Marseille's theatres featured suitably patriotic pieces: *The Dusk of the Boches, the Daughter of the Regiment* and in honour of the Scottish Regiments stationed in the town (and about whom Régina reported) *Bravo the Scots*! The entertainment ended with patriotic singsongs, and numerous performances raised money for the wounded, local hospitals and other 'good works' supporting the war effort. Pleasure would both be – and be seen to be – overlaid with devotion and financial contributions to France's cause.

The civilian population of all of France's main towns and cities was now officially authorised to sing its way to Victory and applaud its beloved poilus as it did so, providing the poilus were heroically represented and no longer the pre-war figures of fun and not always gentle satire.

From Figure of Fun to the Face of Fortitude: Poilus and the changing face of Music Hall

Rudyard Kipling had poeticised the British public's generally scant regard for the common soldier. It is only when 'the guns begin to shoot' that 'Tommy Atkins' becomes 'the saviour of 'is country'. Although France's military system with its conscript army differed from the British volunteer system, by the end of the nineteenth century, the French 'poilu' (equivalent of Britain's Tommy Atkins) had become, as far as his stage representation was concerned, a stock music hall buffoon – if he were from the sun-kissed South and particularly Marseille, the fun verged on cruelty and his defects grossly exaggerated. (Poilus could not be represented in café-concerts due to the prohibitions surrounding the spoken word, costumes and variety acts.)

Mathilde Joseph notes how the British concept of music hall had grown in popularity in France; by the end of the nineteenth century, acts comprised singers, dancers, magicians, performing animals, acrobats and frequently, an inept squaddie who, in the company of scantily-clad ladies, [dis] graced almost every stage. Biting satire as well as bawdy humour were integral to the 'poilu' genre and many other music hall acts; bumbling, at times malicious, good to raise laughs, he was undoubtedly anti-heroic and France would assuredly not seem safe in his hands. Something had to be done to alter the public's perception of their heroic defenders.

When music halls started re-opening from late November 1914, the performance content was strictly controlled and the stage poilu had undergone a makeover. Censors left nothing to chance and as well as the now unacceptable figure of fun, the pre-war satire had to be excised: satire could easily lead to questioning the conduct of the war and nothing could occur on a public stage that might lower morale or jeopardise morality. Enter the solemn, dedicated protector of France's fair fields – arguably as far removed from his flesh and blood alter ego living in the filthy troglodyte world of the trenches as his pre-war counterpart.

Somewhat surprisingly, censors were given few precise guidelines when it came to judging the spoken content of music hall although the 5 August 1914 law, which specifically aimed at repressing journalistic indiscretions in any written form, was deemed applicable to drama. This gave censors considerable freedom to ban or allow pieces that conformed to their personal vision of what was acceptable in terms of morale-boosting, or at least not morale-lowering, content. There appear to have been just two music hall censors; both, according to Joseph, were 'middle-class, mediocre authors themselves of strong religious convictions.' Undeniably 'honest and submissive', they were lacking in 'imagination' – which may or may not have allowed some more subtle pieces to be visée. Joseph quotes Odile Krakovitch's belief that about twenty per cent of offerings were rejected in the month after the music halls re-opened, a figure that dropped to 1.5 per cent by the end of the war. This reduction in visa refusals may have been due to the increasing compliance of, or at least awareness of what would be considered acceptable; censors becoming more relaxed; or the public less willing to have the wool pulled over their eyes about what was happening at the Front.

Joseph suggests that the writers of the approximately 358 music-hall scripts scrutinised during the war adopted a form of self-censorship to increase the likelihood of acquiring that all important visa. Yet, despite writers' need to be acquiescent and offer an acceptable, official view of the war, the public did not see music hall merely as a vehicle for propaganda – which they would probably have rejected and, like café-concerts, they remained popular places of entertainment throughout the war. Perhaps surprisingly, music hall censors were less proscriptive than their song counterparts about how words and gestures were delivered, thereby giving music hall artistes greater flexibility in interpretation (and making scripts harder to evaluate) than lyrics. Thus, whilst we can be sure of how Régina would have performed her songs, we can be less sure of how she might have delivered any spoken music hall pieces.

Irrespective of the venue, even of the city or village in which it was performed, the entertainment would have comprised a mixture of sketches, with at least some featuring the poilu, and variety acts interspersed with songs. The poilu first appeared on stage just as the last notes of the patriotic song, which had opened the evening's entertainment, faded away, leaving the audience in the right mood to cheer this potential saviour of France. Political satire was carefully regulated with the gallant soldier being the most important character. In case any spectator was in doubt about how to respond to events portrayed on stage, the *compère* or *commère* guided their reaction.

When this 'made-over' poilu first strode the boards in early 1915, it was generally in scenes achingly familiar to the audience: the moment of mobilisation and departure for the Front. Accompanied by his loved ones, the stage poilu, like his real-life counterpart, left joyfully for the Front singing 'La Marseillaise' or 'Le Regiment de Sambre et Meuse'; the audience was encouraged to join in, just as many had done as they accompanied loved ones to the station. Occasionally the heroic poilu would be shown returning home wounded, but only in what British poet Siegfried Sassoon cynically referred to as a 'mentionable place'. There was no space on stage for the horrific injuries with which many citizens of Marseille would, even in early 1915, have been agonisingly familiar, their city was by now a big hospital centre for those known as 'gueules cassées' or 'smashed faces'.

If mobilisation had to be portrayed as joyful, and wounds aesthetically pleasing, death could not be totally written out of the script. It was increasingly impossible, even in the make-believe world of music hall, to escape from either the trenches or the high casualty rates but, in terms of the stage, the trenches were sanitised and death 'pour la France' was glorious. Occasionally a supposedly dead poilu was resurrected, to his 'family's' overwhelming joy. Writers' or at least censors' over-arching concern seems to have been to make the poilu and his world seem less inaccessible and spectators feel that they too were involved in the action which reached a climactic finale with processions, music, dancing and of course patriotic songs hailing, as Régina herself did, the Allies. The audience again participated.

Bawdiness, integral to pre-war music hall, also needed to be controlled in the interests of home front morale. Wives, sweethearts and mothers must not be allowed to entertain doubts about how their beloved was spending time out of the Line. Lax behaviour was as unacceptable in music hall as it was in songs. No hint could be made of the army-maintained brothels where women 'serviced' at least eighteen to twenty men a day, even though the women themselves saw this as patriotic work. The poilu might be missing his wife but he would dream chastely of her – as far as his stage persona went.

However popular this early escapism, eventually the public tired of seeing poilus depicted in these quixotic ways. Furthermore, once the real *permissionnaires* began flocking to music halls, there was the danger that they might dispute their idealised portrayal. They wanted to escape the war, not have a stylised view of it thrust upon them. They craved something that 'delighted their eyes' and banished the war to the back of their minds for their precious six days' leave. Beautiful, or at least scantily dressed, women would allow them to forget the horrors of this ever more brutal war in which the poilu realised he was totally expendable (French losses amounted to six million dead, wounded or missing). Extant pictures of Régina held in her file portray her in exotic eveningwear and while her expression might be enticing, it is not lustful.

Inevitably as the war stretched on interminably, the public, although not fully cognisant of the rock-bottom morale amongst many of the French regiments, was progressively war-weary. The tone of the acts changed to reflect this and censors approved songs and scripts that would have been unacceptable in 1915. The theme of the heroic Front disappeared in 1917 following the disastrous April Chemin des Dames offensive, which no amount of press censorship could conceal from the Home Front; naturally the role one Régina Diana may have played was, and would remain, unknown. There had been too many deaths, too much mutilation and too much sacrifice for civilians to be willing to see the war as some glorious game. To survive, music hall had to adapt. The genre's very success lay in its ability to do so. While pessimism remained prohibited, songs and sketches were no longer overwhelmingly confident, espionage stories began to feature, and escapist entertainment replaced the earlier patriotic furore. This ability to reflect the mood of an increasingly demoralised Home Front was one of music hall's strengths. It ensured that audiences accepted that while the fighting man depicted onstage might not represent the whole story, they could still believe in their beloved poilus – at least for the two to three hours the spectacle lasted.

By adapting to the exigencies of wartime in such a way as to continue to attract large, often exuberant audiences, script and song-writers enabled café-concert and music-hall artistes to go on earning their living. Performers and lyricists with a hidden agenda could still mingle with the crowds, glean gossip and information, and report back to their controllers on the struggles taking place on the French Home Front, its belief in the war, its morale, and its citizens' willingness to sing their way to Victory.

Chapter 9

Marseille: City of Sun, Shame and Ships

Marseille: A City in the Sun

Acting almost as a foretaste of things to come, New Year 1914 brought unexpectedly cold, snowy weather to Marseille. Situated deep in the South of France on the Mediterranean Sea, France's oldest city and first port (the Mediterranean's principal and Europe's fourth) generally welcomed in the New Year in temperatures significantly above freezing. One journalist commented in the most widely read local newspaper *Le Petit Provençal* that, slightly to the amusement of their menfolk, women had proved their resourcefulness in their endeavours to clear the snow from a city unused to dealing with extreme weather. He even went so far as to wonder what might have happened to the town without the women. Little could he have known how prophetic his words would become when, once again taken by surprise, Marseille saw her sons leaving for a war none would have anticipated in those cold January days of 1914. Like their counterparts across all combatant nations, the women of Marseille shouldered multiple burdens in both the private and public spheres. Yet a few whose contributions were outwardly patriotic had a hidden agenda, rather than being dedicated to achieving victory, they were actively working for France's defeat.

Marseille, often called the Phoenician City, was founded in the sixth century BC. Throughout French history, its relationship with the rest of France, and particularly monarchist France, was never an easy one; on several occasions in both distant and more recent times, the city had aligned itself with, or sought protection from, France's sworn enemies. According to Marseille historian Olivier Boura, there was even a period during France's post-revolutionary upheavals when obliterating the city was contemplated.

Ironically, in the light of this suggestion, anti-monarchist Marseille had warmly embraced the 1789 Revolution. When, just three years later, Paris was under threat from Austria, a battalion of 517 Marseillais undertook the month-long march to the distant capital and cradle of the Revolution, singing 'Le Chant de guerre de l'Armée du Rhin' as they went. On 10 August 1792, these volunteers from 500 miles away in the far south were key players in the demise of the French monarchy. The words they had intoned came to be considered THE revolutionary song of victory. Re-named *La Marseillaise*, on 14 July 1795 it was dubbed the 'National Hymn'. Variously banned then re-instated, during the 1879 Third Republic it became and has remained the French National Anthem uniting the French and, as happened following the November 2015 Bataclan attacks, even France's allies, in times of crisis. With war on the horizon, on 29 July 1914 the programme of a public concert held in Marseille was abandoned so that the audience could intone its patriotic, defiant words multiple times.

La Marseillaise notwithstanding, as the eighteenth century gave way to the nineteenth, Marseille's troubled relationship with France continued, politically and militarily. Having developed a reputation for religious tolerance, open-mindedness and, vehement opposition to Napoleon III, it was among the first French towns to vote for a socialist municipality – attitudes which did not meet with the approval of France's increasingly right-wing body politic.

Turning to nineteenth century military affairs, soldiers from Marseille, who less than a century ago had flocked to Paris singing their defiance in the face of the Austrian invaders, would in 1870–71 be considered lightweights. They were, many historians argue, falsely accused of not throwing their weight behind the battles which led to the humiliating losses of Alsace and Lorraine. Parisians saw Marseille as 'different', unreliable and, despite its booming industries, 'laid-back'. These issues, which had a profound effect on Marseille and Marseillais in August 1914, were never totally buried.

Whatever the vocal patriotism displayed at the 29 July public concert, the town did not greet the 1 August call to mobilisation with unmitigated enthusiasm. Citizens were not convinced by Prime Minster René Viviani's words 'Moblisation does not mean War' ('la Mobilisation n'est pas la Guerre') appended to the call to arms displayed across France. Nevertheless, those who crowded around the placards shared Marseille's mayor Eugène Pierre's conviction that the local population would support the war effort with the same patriotism and disregard for sacrifice they had always shown in times of trouble. He could not have anticipated the extent to which, in the weeks and months ahead, his co-citizens would be tested both by the enemy within and the enemy without.

As general mobilisation got under way, this generation of recruits belted out the self-same words their forebears had sung when they had headed north for Austrian-threatened Paris in 1792 or Prussian-threatened Sédan in 1870. These currently untested soldiers were as eager as their ancestors to repel this latest German invasion and finally, after forty years, achieve one of France's stated war aims: regain Alsace and Lorraine. Men too old to serve, young boys and women of all ages flocked on to the streets to cheer the soldiers on their way. Singing alongside the entraining men, they were confident that their poilus of the 141ème Régiment d'Infanterie (RI) (Marseille) of the XVème Corps or region whose HQ was at Marseille, consisting primarily of Provençal or Southern troops, would bring honour on their native South and, of course, be home by Christmas. Down at the docks, which would play a key role for the Allies and also Régina Diana and other spies who would soon descend upon Marseille, dockers worked around the clock unloading merchant cargo to make the ships available to the military authorities. Responding to Paris having been placed on a siege footing on 6 August, no light could be shown at night in Marseille, including the lighthouse – just in case enemy zeppelins or ships were in the vicinity. Many felt that this was just precautionary measure. The *der des ders* in the local patois ('guerre des guerres' or war of wars) would not last long leaving Marseille able to resume its profitable day time and nocturnal activities.

These soldiers left behind a city of contrasts, which had benefitted from the rising prosperity of the industrial revolution. The 1906 colonial exhibition had celebrated Marseille's 'Port of Empire' status while the architecture reminded visitors and the Marseillais themselves of the Phoenician City's links with France's many colonies. But Marseille was not only a key trading link with the colonies, it was ideally placed for trade with the Americas and the Far East – making it in wartime the port of choice for incoming troops from around the world, contemporary postcards give a sense of the numbers and variety of troops being processed through Marseille – their provenance and numbers would be of great interest to those instructed to report back to distant Switzerland and thence to Germany on the comings and goings of troops and merchant and military ships, activities which, as her captured postcards make clear, Régina diligently undertook.

Pre-war, Marseille was a melting pot of nationalities drawn by its maritime links. With a population of half a million, it would, in the early days, experience both an exodus of foreigners and ardent protestations of loyalty to France's cause by the approximately 110,000 resident Italians (eighty-five per cent of the total foreign population), some of whom would join the French Foreign legion before Italy entered the war (May 1915). Despite the various nationalities having previously co-existed peacefully, waves of anti-German feelings soon shook the city, fuelled by a xenophobic press which would exhort readers to spurn and distrust everyone and all things

German – including beer – and treat with suspicion any Marseillais against whom an accusation of not being one hundred per cent pro-France and her allies could be levied. As happened in England, long-standing residents and families with Germanic-sounding names or German accents when speaking French, some of whose sons were already serving with the French colours, were vilified. Tensions rapidly ran high.

Jean-Yves Le Naour notes how spy-fever also gripped the town. Censors scanned the papers for potential hidden messages in small ads columns; the right-wing *Le Petit Marseillais* (readership approximately 200,000) warned the population to be on its guard against potential agents of the Kaiser, even tramps and the homeless were suspect. To deflect suspicion, agents spying for Germany would need French-sounding names and native accents. Bizarrely, higher-ranking French officers in uniform were accused of being Germans in disguise and attacked; as Régina's story shows, even genuine French officers were capable of (unintentionally) divulging information. Feelings ran so high that Germans and Austrians now wishing, or forced by conscription, to return to their native lands had to be given police and even infantry protection. In this volatile atmosphere, singing soldiers and their families continued to march to the St Charles station; mobilisation took ten days to complete. If the poilus themselves were worried that the war would be over before they got there, many mothers, wives, sisters, fiancées and children feared they were embracing their loved one for the last time for, by the time the last conscript headed north, it was painfully obvious that all was not going well at the Front.

As the final wave of mobilisation was completed, news reports and then trains carrying soldiers the other way began to arrive in Marseille, the first on 15 August. Whatever *Le Petit Marseillais* may have said about wounds being 'superficial' and the wounded desperate to return to the battlefields, those who witnessed the arrival of these first of hundreds of thousands of casualties to descend upon Marseille during the next four years may have begged to differ. Arrivals on 16 and 21 August provided terrifying evidence of the damage a machine gun could wreak on the human frame. Although the French Military High Command had, in April 1914, assured infantry regiments that 'the will to conquer alone assures success', those who faced a hail of shrapnel and machine-gun fire would have begged to differ. Amongst the dissenters was a young lieutenant named Charles de Gaulle; wounded at Dinant in Belgium on 15 August, he wrote how all the courage in the world is insufficient against mighty fire-power.

Before long, Marseille's three pre-war hospitals were unable to cope, schools and convents were requisitioned, and twenty-two convalescent homes would be established. Marseille became the leading centre for 'les gueles cassées' (as those suffering from horrific facial wounds were called) as well as several hospitals specialising in amputations and rehabilitation workshops in which women were closely involved. As in all belligerent countries, hospitals were dependent upon women fund-raisers and volunteers to provide additional resources for the medical authorities were stretched to breaking point. Concerts were staged specifically to raise funds for the hospitals; patriotic artistes generously offered their services.

The Marseille town council rallied both spiritually and financially behind the medical effort. It was hoped that the city's sunny climate would assist soldiers' recuperation and, as the war lengthened, daily walks to nearby beauty spots were organised, with heavily subsidised refreshments available, 10 centimes per cup of tea, coffee, chocolate. Preserved photographs show convalescents accompanied by female volunteers sunning themselves or walking along the beach. Women with a few hours to spare could engage in the patriotic activity of assisting the recovery of those wounded 'pour la France'.

Associations were formed which provided entertainment for the convalescents, many taking advantage of Marseille's benign climate. In 1916, the local Ramblers' Association (Société des Excursionistes Marseillais) rented the ten acre open space, La Calèche. Approximately one hundred convalescents were entertained there every day, volunteer nurses accompanying the most severely wounded. Along with card games, gentle walks and sunbathing, artistes provided musical entertainments; meals and delicacies were provided – the 35 centimes per person per day cost was funded by a continuous round of fund-raising. The Provence Tourist Offices provided 'an abundant distribution of beer' (quickly re-instated after the initial anti-Germanic feelings) and Marseille's women generously offered sweets, flowers, cigarettes and a listening ear to men long deprived of sympathetic female companionship.

Preserved photographs in her file demonstrate soldiers related easily to Régina. There is no indication that the Calèche volunteers were vetted and, in Régina's case, what could arouse suspicion? A Swiss resident with an Italian passport, a French mother, a daughter in Crest, a powerful singing voice and an established reputation as a 'chanteuse lyrique' would have been undoubtedly warmly welcomed. Yet the information that she was instructed to amass relating to the numbers of wounded, the extent of their injuries, their regiments, names of the battlefields where injuries were sustained and the morale among both troops and civilians (which decreased as the cost of living as well as the numbers of casualties increased) was being pieced together to build up a larger picture of the all-important 'home front'.

Marseille was not only heaving with wounded. Its well-established reputation as a welcoming city and its geographical situation far from the Front – resented by those living closer to the battle lines – made it the ideal place of refuge for the hundreds of thousands of often traumatised Belgian and other refugees from the North and East of France who had fled the advancing German Armies. Marseille's financial accounts for 1915 indicate that the city spent over eleven million francs on those unflatteringly termed 'useless mouths' ('bouches inutiles'), their numbers soon swollen by other nationalities and without the generosity and financial support of private citizens, refugees in Marseille would have lived in abject poverty. Once the novelty of welcoming refugees diminished, parts of the local press did indeed see these hapless individuals as a drain on the city's resources and some dubbed them as 'shirkers who had got out of fighting' or even 'the Boches of the North'. While their own sons were fighting and dying in the North of France, feeding, housing and providing free concerts for refugees struck some Marseillais as a patriotic duty too far and there were rumblings of discontent – of great interest to spymasters. Wars are not won on the battlefield alone.

Marseille: A Shamed City

At the same time as the wounded were flooding into Marseille in August 1914, troops of the Southern regions' XVème Corps fighting in the Lorraine area were, just like the young lieutenant Charles de Gaulle in Dinant, discovering the inadequacies of will-power and patriotism when confronted by a well-equipped and superbly organised enemy. This would scar Marseille, its reactions to, and its relations with, France until the bitter end. The City of Sun was being transformed into a City of Shame which would henceforth strive to negate the slander heaped upon it by the Parisian press abetted by the French government and High Command. The sad story is briefly told, but its echoes and repercussions would have interested German agents and their handlers.

A burning desire to avenge the humiliating 1870 loss of Alsace and parts of Lorraine, rendered the French High Command desperate to regain these so-called 'twin daughters'. For a few euphoric hours on 8 August 1914, this appeared to have occurred. Mulhouse, taken without a shot being fired, was back in French hands. Newspapers were jubilant. However, hints that all was not going as well at the Front as initially reported, soon appeared.

The Germans had successfully counter-attacked. On 10 August, the (predominantly Marseillais) men of the 141ème RI had undergone a baptism of more than fire. With bayonets fixed and unsupported by heavy artillery, they were mown down by the strength of the German firepower including the Maschinenegewehr 08; four days later, further disasters engulfed the Provençal troops. Then on 19 August, General Castelnau sent the XVème Corps into an attack at Dieuze. With no artillery cover, they were thrown against positions that Germany had been fortifying for the forty-odd years since it occupied the Moselle area. Still today at 'Kilometre 0', reinforced concrete German bunkers and blockhaus bear witness to the strength of the German fortifications in the occupied provinces. Certain of the Southern Corps' companies lost eighty per cent of their strength. Withdrawal was inevitable. Castelnau, a firm believer in the 'offensive spirit' doctrine, sacked the leaders whom he considered responsible for the disaster – which did not help the dead. One French soldier poet from Provence (killed at Verdun in 1916) believed that, for the casualties at least, 'These golden words will be remembered for evermore/Dieuze glorious tomb of the 15th Corps' [Ces mots seront gravés en belles letters d'or/Dieuze, tombeau glorieux du 15ème Corps] quoted in Claude Camous. His hope would soon be proven a vain one.

The 22 August military communiqué noted significant French losses in the face of (and this was stressed) the enemy's superior manpower – twice that estimated by French strategists and intelligence officers. Incandescent with rage, and refusing to believe that the enemy had outnumbered and outgunned the French troops, Minister for War Adolphe Messimy threatened to shoot the generals responsible for the retreat. When it was pointed out that this was an unhelpful solution, nor would the use of the guillotine resolve the situation, he sought a stooge. His eye alighted on the troops from the warm, laidback and 'amiable' south, with the history of bad blood stretching back into both distant and recent history.

Re-igniting prejudices of the previous century when as well as being accused of being poor soldiers, Marseillais were deemed politically left-wing, 'insolent and presumptuous', represented on the Parisian stage as buffoon-like stereotypes stepping straight out of the librettos of their beloved Rossini operas, Messimy knew where to direct his ire. To re-enforce his case, nineteenth century science was invoked to demonstrate that, softened by the sun, those who lived in warm climates lacked steel in their souls. Thus it was argued, France's international and national concerns, including the regaining of Alsace Lorraine, counted little in the distant, sun-drenched

Midi. Geographically perched in its detractors' eyes at the edge of France, Marseillais, with their comical accents and laid-back attitudes, were, in the opinion of much of the rest of the country, hardly even French.

The Phoenician City had barely begun to mourn the death or wounding (within a mere four days) of 12,500 (forty-two per cent) of the 30,000 men and 220 (forty per cent) of the 550 officers, she had sent to the Front (1,400 combatants were killed during the night of 19–20 August alone) when an article appeared in France's second largest circulation newspaper *Le Matin* (Paris). Dated 24 August, written by Auguste Gervais, a Senator from the Seine and friend of Messimy, it was obvious that the scapegoat had been found. The article, which ran like wildfire across France, would inflict immeasurable, long-lasting damage on the men of the South and particularly Marseille. It would affect their relationship with Northern France and Paris throughout the war and well beyond. Omitting all mention of the lack of heavy ammunition, the failings of Joffre, Castelnau and Foch, the dearth of intelligence, the article claimed that the loud-mouthed sun-softened soldiers from what was sneeringly referred to as 'aimable Provence' had panicked in the face of the enemy, let down those in the line adjacent to them, taken to their heels and fled. The article demanded that the full weight of military law be invoked against officers and men of the XVème whose actions had apparently led to the debacle and loss of French honour. French politician Abel Ferry, who had been fighting in the Verdun sector, wrote to his wife on 3 September that he would personally willingly shoot 200 men from each Southern regiment – this would supposedly turn the remainder into 'superb troops' ('troupes superbes')!

The citizens and press of Marseille and the other equally implicated Southern départments (including Corsica, which had of course given France her greatest solider and the world one of its greatest military minds, namely Napoléon Bonaparte), erupted in fury. Recognising that the article was, if not penned by, then at least prompted by Messimy himself (otherwise it would not have been cleared by the censors), Provençal politicians demanded an audience with the Minister. His refusal added insult to injury. As far as the South was concerned, Gervais, Messimy and the 'treasonable actions' of the Parisian press had jeopardised, possibly even destroyed, the Union Sacrée which politicians had demanded of all French citizens barely three weeks before. In its riposte, the Marseille newspaper *Le Soleil* accused Senator Gervais of high treason for attempting to divide rather than unite the nation; *Le Petit Marseillais* echoed these sentiments. *Le Matin* was banned in Marseille and beyond. Complaints from its owners about the loss of business fell on deaf ears; they were reminded of the additional agony that the article had heaped on the heartbroken families of the dead, missing and wounded. So febrile was the atmosphere that the cheese manufacturer Charles Gervais witnessed plummeting sales and attempted formally to dissociate his family from the Senator whose name they had the misfortune to share (*Le Petit Provençal* 30 August 1914). To little avail, it was months before customers returned.

As if the article were not calumny enough, a fortnight later, the Marseille Chief of Police received a telegram from the General Staff informing him that a significant number of men of the XVème had absconded and returned to their homes. Gendarmes were ordered to carry out 'in-depth searches' and arrest the culprits who would be tried by military tribunal. The whole of Marseille felt it was being sacrificed on the altar of public opinion. An audience with the Minister having once again been refused, local and national politicians from Provence published an open letter condemning the French War Office and demanding an apology. The breach in the Union Sacrée was fast becoming a rupture.

While agreeing wholeheartedly with the sentiments expressed and grateful for the support offered by other mayors even from distant towns such as Lyon, Marseille mayor, Eugène Pierre, pleaded for calm. The Bouches-du-Rhone MP, Auguste Eugène César Marie Bouge, confronted Gervais directly, tauntingly inviting him to visit the hospitals and cemeteries where the men of this easy-going South now lay. He damningly accused him, at this moment of crisis in France's history where she was fighting for her very survival, of playing directly into the enemy's hands – of being a 'collaborator' (Camous). The local press taunted Messimy with being an 'armchair soldier' and wondered how he could have the effrontery to believe that he was qualified to teach lessons to those in the field.

Realising the scale of the mistake and the depth of the fury they had unleashed, both Gervais and Messimy undertook damage limitation. In an article published in *Le Figaro* Messimy distanced himself from Gervais but his days in power were strictly numbered. Prime Minister René Viviani replaced him as Minister of War with the more effective Alexandre Millerand. Gervais was forced to retract and issue, if not an apology, then a statement that while some soldiers from the South may have been derelict in their duty, the same could not be said of the whole regiment. This was seen in Marseille as too little too late, and neither civilians nor soldiers were prepared to forgive those who had vilified the regiment and its men.

Six months later, the heroic death of 36-year-old Frédéric Chevillon, mayor of the nearby town of Allauch and representative in the National Chamber of Deputies went some way to calming the waters. On 21 February 1915 at Eparges, south-east of Verdun, seemingly determined to avenge the reputation of his southern comrades, he reportedly shouted 'you will see how we die in the XVème Corps' as he led his men out of the trench into a volley of German fire. Alexandre Millerand led the tributes to this 5th Deputy to die at the Front. Millerand's condolence telegram to Frédéric's sister assured her that representing all 'les enfants du Midi' (children of the South of France), the Bouches-du-Rhone deputy had fought gloriously on the fields of France and he, like so many others, had given his life for 'la patrie'. *Le Matin,* the paper where the scandal had originated, was quick to heap praise on Chevillon and blame Messimy for his part in the sordid affair of six months ago. Some Marseillais were prepared to accept the olive branch of peace, feeling that their men and Corps had finally been vindicated and rejoice that the Union Sacrée was still (just) intact. Others, particularly the more left-wing press was far from appeased and riposted that nothing *Le Matin* did or said could undo the damage done, nor the foul taste left in the mouths of those from the Midi and especially the Bouches-du-Rhone. Alexandre Millerand had had enough. On 25 February 1915, he ordered censors to use their blue pencil whenever mention was made of the 141ème. For good or ill, neither the Regiment nor its men were to figure in the press. As far as Marseille was concerned, this meant that the falsehoods of August 1914 would remain their soldiers' legacy and whatever their valour, they feared that they were powerless to counter the charges.

These fears appear to have been well founded. Those serving in small groups in non-southern regiments often found themselves ostracised; many soldiers claimed that they were frequently at the back of the queue for medical treatment when wounded, accused of malingering, of self-inflicting wounds (and shot or imprisoned for these only for evidence later to reveal the fallacy of the accusation), returned to active duty far sooner than they should have been, and, following the mutinies of 1917 triggered in part at least by the Chemin des Dames debacle in which Régina played a part, proportionately more southern troops were executed 'for the sake of example' than those from other areas of France. The reputation given to the 141ème in a vicious Parisian newspaper article in August 1914 which had spread across France, thus had a profound effect on the Phoenician City and her sons' reputation throughout, and indeed well beyond, the war.

It was this traumatised city, perched on the edge of France yet the Southern gateway both to the battlefields of the North and the Mediterranean theatres of war, that German spymasters had in their sights. There would be much to keep agents occupied and many roles, including seemingly highly patriotic ones, which they could assume to hide their activities from prying eyes, ones in which Régina excelled.

'Is there not a letter for me?' Wartime godmothers

Like their British and German counterparts, the French military authorities had anticipated a quick and victorious war, the need to sustain troops' morale over a lengthy conflict had not figured in their preparations. However, as the fronts became gridlocked and the troops dug in, it became increasingly obvious that one group of men were suffering an additional morale-lowering anguish. While their comrades regularly received letters, parcels and loving messages from their families, those whose homes and loved ones were trapped in the areas of France under enemy occupation received nothing. For many of them, the daily distribution of the post became almost unbearable, one even going so far as to confess, 'it's all I can do not to cry.'

Although few sources credit Marseille with having had the original idea, in late 1914, aware that his city was unable to shake off all the accusations levelled against it, and deeply aware of soldiers' feelings of isolation, journalist Jean Faber of the *Petit Marseillais* developed a novel idea. Marseille and her women could act as 'marraines' (godmothers) to both soldiers and towns in the war zone. (The adoption of a town would be put on hold until the closing weeks of hostilities and stretched well into the post-bellum years.)

Jean Faber was not alone in his concern for the lonely soldiers. In January 1915, a lady of strong religious beliefs and impeccable virtue, Mlle Marguerite de Lens, helped by the newspaper *l'Echo de Paris*, established an organisation that would enable all Frenchwomen including of course Marseillaises to express their solidarity with the troops. Named 'La Famille du Soldat' (Soldier's Family) an army of 'marraines' would keep up the morale of a soldier 'filleul' (godson) to whom she would write and send comforts, giving him the sense of a family who cared about him in the rear. The idea was contagious. Françoise Thébaud believes 25,000 men applied to become 'filleuls'. 'La Famille du Soldat' was soon followed by 'Mon Soldat', organised by a similarly devout Mme Bérard with the support of Alexandre Millerand; 6,000 additional men applied for a 'marraine'. The very name with its religious connotations made the idea appear lofty and patriotic. Certificates were issued to both parties and correspondence was quickly established. By the end of the war, this touching enterprise had been tainted by scandal, with the 'marraines' accused of espionage and prostitution.

Irrespective of how detractors finally came to view this epistolary movement that involved women from across France and beyond, it was of crucial importance and brought comfort to thousands of men in the trenches, to women on the Home Front and to men on the high seas who also sought 'marraines', (often giving contact details in Marseille, their ship's home port); many women treasured the letters and cards they received from their 'godson' or indeed 'godsons' and were deeply saddened if the worst occurred. One 'marraine', 'Alice', preserved the postcards she exchanged with several of her godsons from the Savoy region of France, one of whom spent some time in Marseille and was serving with the 141ème RI. The cards, which become increasingly warm in tone, give detailed information about where each correspondent's regiment was camped, where they were going, on what date, and indeed their route. These postcards contained information that would have been of great interest had they fallen into the wrong hands.

There is ample evidence that Marseille women continued to embrace this role first mooted in one of their local papers and which further demonstrated their patriotism. Some Marseillaises took Zouaves (French colonial soldiers) under their wing as Malik Brouri confirms in his 28 April 1915 diary entry. Given a few hours leave, he meets up with a 40-year-old widow, Marie, he is delighted she has agreed to be his 'marraine de guerre'. The eagerness of French women of all social backgrounds (thus increasing the idea of the Union Sacrée which had taken such a battering in Marseille in August 1914), of varying literacy skills and ages, ranging from little girls to those disparagingly referred to as 'old maids', elderly women and bereaved mothers, to become involved was replicated in neutral countries where significant numbers of women applied for a French godson. By 1917, the Parisian broadsheet *Le Figaro*, which had thrown its weight behind the idea in 1915, was so overwhelmed with requests from putative godmothers and godsons that it had to remind readers that it was a newspaper and not a vehicle for small advertisements.

Not all applications were as harmless as the devout Catholic initiators had intended. Some relationships rapidly moved beyond the control of the founding organisations, nor did all the pairings live up to the lofty religious ideals that the word 'godmother' implies. Soon a plethora of newspapers were offering to link those serving their country at the front with the women who were keeping the home fires burning; on 1 May 1915, the low-brow, humorous, fortnightly *Fantasio* published 'The Flirt on the Front' – the title says it all. The ensuing requests to *Fantasio* were so overwhelming that the magazine could not keep up, and abandoned the listings in November. On 4 December 1915, the widely read, bawdy *La Vie Parisienne* (advertisements initially cost 2 francs rising in 1918 to 4 francs) picked up *Fantasio's* torch, seemingly less worried about the volume of requests which soon covered two pages, perhaps seeing that these made good financial sense. The magazine became known as the war's great Matrimonial (or even pimping) Agency. One wonders what spymasters in neutral Switzerland, busily culling their enemies' papers for information including that contained in the small ads, made of this glut of requests for contact between the home and the Front and how many of their protégées were encouraged to offer epistolary godmotherly services. There is firm evidence that with French newspapers widely available in the French-speaking cantons, many women in francophone Switzerland adopted the role, for the most part innocently. Swiss women eagerly strove to alleviate the sufferings of those in belligerent countries. In February 1916, fearful that spies may be masquerading as godmothers, the French Military authorities banned all Swiss applicants; anxieties of this turning into a diplomatic incident meant that the interdiction had no sooner been passed than the French government lifted it.

By the time this short-lived ban was introduced, considerable confusion surrounded the role of all 'marraines', not just those from neutral countries. Alexandre Millerand alerted French censors of the need to be ultra-vigilant with the letters of 'marraines' for fear that some of the women recruited via the Small Ads sections might be spies working in France. There was a feeling that once friendly communication and postcard exchanges were well established, officers and men would let down their guards and might communicate information potentially beneficial to the enemy, this is certainly apparent in some of Régina's correspondence.

All communications sent to Poste Restante addresses were to be destroyed, and the patriotic right-wing press vilified one Poste Restante provider as being simultaneously an outlet for pimps and for German spies. Certainly spies (not perforce 'marraines') sending information to Switzerland used PR addresses until the Swiss authorities banned them. Closer to the mark than they realised, the newspaper *L'Intransigeant* even claimed that France had been militarily defeated by 'pornographic small ads' acting as a cover for German spies and blames, partly at least, 'pimping' godmother spies for the failure of the April 1917 Chemin des Dames offensive. The 'Service des Renseignements Militaire' began to insert false advertisements in the hopes of catching German spies – seemingly unsuccessfully. *L'Intransigeant* praised British perspicacity in forbidding such relationships and banning their troops from applying for a French 'marraine'. Who, the paper wondered, knew what nefarious information was being concealed in this correspondence between a man and a woman whom the fortunes of war had thrown together? In Régina's case at least, a great deal.

By early 1917 with the previously much lauded patriotic 'marraines' facing significant opprobrium, fewer women were willing to become involved; the same cannot be said of those wishing to become godsons. On 28 June 1917, the Commander of the French Armies of the North and East, Robert Nivelle, formally requested the Minister for War to put an end to the practice; the request was refused. Despite commanders' on-going angst about 'marraines' and their godsons, Millerand still felt that overall the practice was too popular to ban.

Unsurprisingly, the role in all its complexity found its way not only onto postcards but into (not always complimentary) novels and plays, music hall acts, and songs, where, as Régina Sweeney points out, the sexual as well as idealised role of the marraine simply became part of wartime culture. Surprisingly in the light of the censors' mission to safeguard morality, some (although far from all) songs went so far as to hint at what the marraine might offer her poilu when he came home on leave. 'La Marraine des Poilus', 'Chère Marraine', 'L'Idylle du Poilu' and many others acquired that all important visa. Several cultural historians argue that with the authorities' increasing anxieties about the slaughter of young Frenchmen, marraines were even seen as patriotically re-stocking the nation. It is tempting to believe that some of the postcards used as evidence in Régina's trial were from a soldier who saw himself as her godson. The relationship could easily have begun this way as relatively formal exchanges soon give way to familiar ones, even expressions of devotion from 'your kid', the cards thus following the normal development of this very particular relationship. Régina may well have sung either the popular 'La Réponse de la Marraine' or one of the more risqué numbers in her performances, confirming her adherence to the French cause and her embracing all aspects of a Frenchwoman's patriotic duty to sustain a man at the front, while simultaneously duplicitously luring men to their deaths.

There is no doubt that 'marrainage' was just one of the many ways that a singer from a neutral francophone country could blend seamlessly into the war effort. A port such as Marseille with its numerous places of entertainment, constant influx of troops, seamy side and its all-encompassing need to appear ultra-patriotic, provided an artiste with an additional hidden agenda with fertile spying ground, cast-iron reasons for exchanging postcards with soldiers, and a backdrop against which she could become all but invisible.

Postcards and Prostitutes

Still today second-hand markets regularly take place in towns and villages across France; among the most popular stalls are those selling postcards. Collectors and sellers engage in deep discussions with both parties often being highly knowledgeable. Carefully arranged into 'départments' and themes, the lost provinces of Alsace and Lorraine often have a whole section of their own. Images invariably depict an idealised, feminised or infantilised view of the region with either bucolic peasants or, more frequently, charming young women or children clad in traditional costumes, often waving a French flag. In countless contemporary Alsace/Lorraine cards, the woman is embracing a poilu who will be instrumental in forging 'La Réunion'. These appear to have been among the most popular wartime postcards in France; one in my collection was sent from the Bouches-du-Rhone, thus Marseille area of France.

In the century before Facebook, Twitter, and the internet, postcards were the ubiquitous way of sending quick and cheap messages to friends and family. The first (non-picture) postcards originated in Austria in October 1869 with illustrated ones appearing the following year – German ones were of particularly high quality. In the early days, the French were reluctant to embrace what was considered a 'Prussian invention', but when the postcard craze hit France in 1873 senders made up for lost time. Over 300,000 copies of an image of the Eiffel Tower were sold to visitors to the 1889 Paris Exposition Universelle, doing much to popularize the format. The first French tourist view postcard intended for dispatch rather than a souvenir, was produced in Marseille in 1891. By 1914 postcards were ubiquitous. A plethora of French images of World War One still exist; pictures of regiments, matériel and personnel abound, faces frozen forever when the shutter clicked. What is fascinating about these French postcards is the amount of visual information that they can reveal.

In a country where every word in a song had to meet the censor's approval, it is surprising to see the number of postcards available in Marseille showing the names of foreign regiments, their dates of arrival at the port and images of troops embarking on war ships with the name clearly visible. My copy of 'Les Troupes Russes à Marseille 20 Avril 1916 (Russian troops at Marseille

1916)' was sent by a woman signing herself 'votre petite amie Marseillaise Aimée' (who may perhaps appear on the postcard as she has circled the depicted nurse with her own name). The information that these 11,000 troops had received a delirious welcome after their sixty-day, 30,000km journey and were, according to the contemporary *L'Illustration*, hailed as the 'rouleau compresseur russe' (the Russian road roller) which would crush the Germans, would have interested any spy handler. Other popular postcards show crowds cheering *inter alia* troops from New Zealand, South Africa and a contingent of Ravi Lancers as they paraded on separate occasions through the city. Postcards also reveal how men from the Indian Army were camped at the Parc Borély, early British arrivals bivouacked at the Camp de St Marcel while Hôpital Auxiliare 2 in Marseille boasted a sophisticated X-ray unit. Although what was written on cards could be censored, photographic images were seemingly not subject to the same scrutiny. We will never know the complete set of images Régina and the other army of spies working in Marseille sent back to their handlers, but they certainly had ample choice.

Not all cards depicted military scenes. In France as in England, sentimental wartime pictures were also freely available: marraines dreaming of their adopted soldier godsons, children praying for their father's safe return, wives thinking longingly of their fighting husbands, mothers knitting love and luck into every stich of the sock they are making, but at this point the images diverge. Although many slightly bawdy English First World War cards exist, they are along the lines of 'naughty seaside postcard' humour; few are as openly risqué, even pornographic, as the French ones.

France had long been considered less squeamish about women euphemistically termed 'filles de joie' (good time girls) than Great Britain and if poilus' patriotic duty was to re-stock the nation, there were plenty of women available to help them acquire or refine the necessary skills. An internet search for postcard images of 'prostitutes in Marseille 1914–1918' led to thirty-six 'hits' on an international postcard site, not one hit was returned when Portsmouth was substituted for Marseille nor even when only the search term 'prostitute' was entered. Perhaps surprising, at least to the more prudish Anglo-Saxon mind, is the amount of information that French deltiology reveals about the world's 'oldest profession'. A number of preserved postcards, both hand-drawn and photographic, dating from the years immediately preceding and during the war, depict ports (including Marseille) where soldiers, sailors and civilians can be seen checking out the local talent and inevitably many cards are entitled 'manoeuvres de nuit' (night manoeuvres). Ribald postcards are thus a useful source of information about the world in which Régina lived, however discreetly, even if this were not her sole occupation. There is significant evidence that she had several close 'amis', (male friends) some perhaps initially met in a café-concert, lingering at the dock or even in one of the carefully regulated 'maison close' (brothels) which were tolerated across France.

Turning the clock back to the early nineteenth century, although Napoleon had tried to regulate the civilian sex industry, a 'Service des Moeurs' (Morals Unit) was only established in France and a series of rules initiated in 1843. Brothels could not be situated in residential areas, had to proclaim their line of business by displaying both the house number and a red lamp (during the war, a blue light indicated that the house was restricted to officers); the Grand Hotel des Princes, Marseille, where Régina entertained her lover and received some of her mail was requisitioned for officers, and windows had to be shuttered. The 'madame' had to be female – many were themselves former prostitutes. Postcards invariably reflect these regulations – those depicting exteriors frequently portray groups of soldiers and sailors flocking to the door and those concentrating on the interior show the 'good time' available inside. Sweeney argues that in the minds of the French authorities there was a belief that sexual activity increased a man's virility and aggression and therefore 'les filles de joie' were helping the war effort!

By 1917, French military doctor and specialist in venereal diseases, Alfred Anzoulay, had noted that prostitutes were everywhere, his long list of places where they passed unnoticed due to their sheer numbers included café-concerts as well as theatres, the precise world in which Régina moved. He was far from the only specialist or military man to voice such concerns.

Eventually the French High Command was so concerned about the prevalence of both Sexually Transmitted Diseases and the possibility of spies doubling up as prostitutes, that the military began running 'Bordel Militiares de Campagne' (Military Campaign Brothels), sometimes subcontracting to a local pimp. These sprang up near training camps and other zones with large concentrations of soldiers, local prostitutes were often forced to leave the area. French BMC were of course only available to French military personnel although similar provision was made for British and Dominion forces. The Americans were less tolerant towards those who were, as it was euphemistically termed, 'missing their wives.'

Whilst Anzoulay and the French High Command were harbouring concerns about STDs and spies, extant information about Elisabeth Schragmüller indicates that the morals or indeed sexual health of those whom she recruited were of no interest to her, her guiding force was the information that they could glean and transmit. Her pre-war experience as a social worker may have helped her to understand the profile and financial needs of women working the ports, selling sexual favours to often desperately lonely and vulnerable men. She had no qualms about recruiting 'good time girls' whose own moral code would have allowed them, as it allowed Régina, to lure men to their bed and take careful note of all that they might unburden about life at or near the front, the ships they might be about to board and, where known, their ultimate destination.

Marseille was no exception to the open prostitution that flourished across wartime France. Before the war it was already the most renowned French port in terms of the sex trade. According to Stephan Likosky between 1872 and 1882 there were 3,584 registered and unknown numbers of unregistered sex workers, the number increased exponentially in the ensuing decades. The reputations of some of France's greatest late nineteenth century, early twentieth century painters (Picasso, Manet, Toulouse-Lautrec and Dégas) owed much to their portrayal of 'les filles de joie'.

Turning to the war itself, using Marseille archives Le Naour argues that hundreds of 'girls' evacuated from the North made their way to Marseille and continued their business in the great Mediterranean port. Pierre Louis Buzzi's research shows that many from the Toul area (North Eastern France) were 'sent' to Marseille. This influx of women from other areas would have allowed Régina to pass, and continue to pass, unnoticed when she first arrived in March 1915. As early as 23 June 1916 *Le Petit Provençal* was outraged at this further sullying of Marseille's reputation demanding that the morality police take drastic action – which they did, albeit not always successfully and occasionally even embarrassingly, by arresting innocent high-ranking women whose virtue was beyond reproach. The police appear to have been either unable or unwilling to control the situation, Le Naour has calculated that by June 1918 there were at least 8,000 women working the town – most of them passing beneath the medical military authority's radar. He adds that in one road alone in the Red Light district there were some fifteen establishments with between four and eleven women apiece.

Despite the outrage of newspapers and many upstanding citizens at the city's seemingly justified reputation for immorality, the continuous arrival and departure of hundreds of thousands of military personnel meant that prostitution became accepted as a necessary – at least from the soldiers' and sailors' point of view – part of life. In bars, parks, theatres and places of public entertainment, and, if the postcards are to be believed, roads near the Old Port, sex workers openly propositioned soldiers of different ethnicities who, for the most part, willingly parted with a few sous to help them to forget what they had just been through or what might be to come. Those at the higher end of the scale than the women depicted in a rather heart-wrenching 1918 series of cards depicting this area, could earn a good living and just as the military authorities had feared, with a little judicious questioning, acquire and share information helpful to the enemy. Both before and during the war, women like Régina who were of doubtful, albeit relatively discreet immorality, would have simply blended into the background in this port where sex was in the air. Blending in or being invisible is the first requirement of a spy.

Port City and Sunken Ships

Like many of her contemporaries, British Territorial Forces Nursing Sister, Ethel Burgess (1885–1970) kept a diary of her war service. In late November 1917, she left England for France; arriving in Marseille on 3 December, she and her nursing colleagues were ashore awaiting onward transport for Alexandria, their ultimate destination. Seemingly an experienced well-travelled nurse, she noted on 7 December 1917: 'We are warned to be very careful as the place is full of spies i.e. Marsailles [sic]'. Furthermore, 'we are not allowed out alone but must go in two's and three's during the day or in fours and sixes after dark.' Her unfavourable view of Marseille, shared by many of her colleagues, was undoubtedly coloured by the uncomfortable living conditions they were experiencing, 'We are sleeping in tents and it is very cold', as they waited to set sail on HMT *Aragon*.

Despite Burgess' observation about 'spies', she may not have been fully aware that enemy spies in Marseille had long been busy observing all Allied shipping; they almost certainly had the self-same *Aragon* on which she and her colleagues would sail fifteen days later in their sights as she had already been anchored off Marseille for two weeks. Torpedoed on 30 December within sight of Alexandria Harbour, *Aragon* sank in under fifteen minutes. Of the 2,100 souls on board, 604 Commonwealth officers and men, and six VADs perished.

By the time *Aragon* was lost in December 1917, Régina herself was no longer at liberty to spy on ships at anchor or leaving Marseille – although others in her ring were. As several ships are cited in her trial and were fundamental to the prosecution's case, recounting the detailed story of just one of the vessels she is known to have spied upon and reported information to her handlers about puts the human face on her and her network's activities.

On 3 May 1917, only weeks after Régina had herself ceased to be active but her ring still was, HMT *Transylvania* left Marseille bound, seemingly unbeknownst to the troops, for Alexandria. Amongst the 3,400 souls aboard were RAMC Lieutenant Philip Murphy, TFNS Sister Jessie Clementia Hayward and Sergeant Walter Williams (905 Motor Transport Coy, Army Service Corps). The vivid memories of 92-year-old Williams were captured seventy years later in two (of five) sound recordings held at the Imperial War Museum. Their individual accounts of when the ship was sunk by two torpedoes some five miles off the Italian coast in the Bay of Genoa, on 4 May 1917 are graphic and remain deeply moving a century later.

When Sergeant Williams from Weston-super-Mare travelled by train to Marseille in late April 1917, he was a veteran of the Western Front. On the morning of 3 May, he, his men and their Peerless lorries, which he considered 'slow but very efficient', left their quarters at Camp Carcassone just outside Marseille and 'in glorious sunshine', reached the port. He remembered being watched by a group of German prisoners working on the docks who exchanged 'leering glances' and made signs 'as though we were swimming'. With hindsight, Williams wondered if the prisoners knew something that the men and women embarking on the ship did not. According to Williams, *Transylvania* a 14,600 ton former Cunard passenger ship belonging to the Anchor Line was 'the biggest ship to sail the Mediterranean'. She was a 'very fine ship' with sufficient quarters for every person on board to have their own bed – quite rare on army transports. Two Japanese destroyers, for whose crew Williams would be effusive in his praise, convoyed her. Once aboard, Williams recalled there was, 'much to do', lifebelts were distributed and the first full ship's complement lifeboat drill was scheduled for 10am the following day. This would prove to be a fatal error.

Following a calm night, the whistle blew 'for parade' just before 10am; personnel headed for the deck. They included Lt Philip Murphy who remembered how a 'cursed torpedo c[a]me towards us from about a distance of 300 yards'. This was German U-boat, U-63, commanded by the highly decorated Commander Otto Schultze. Initially mesmerised, Murphy, 'could not believe my eyes but very soon I realised that what I saw was only too real.' Both Murphy and Williams note that the first torpedo hit *Transylvania* in the engine room, killing some of the crew. The ship, five miles off the shore, came to an immediate standstill, according to eyewitness accounts and also the long poem 'The Loss of the *Transylvania*' by Geo. J. M. Mabbott of 906 Company Motor Transport, Army Service Corps (MTASC).

Up rose a shout, what did it mean?
The women all were saved
Two boats, filled with the sisters true
Launched and good-byes waved.

These 'sisters true' were the sixty-six QAIMNS, TFNS and three VAD nurses (the kit of one more sister had been erroneously embarked while she herself fortuitously remained ashore). Had the ship being carrying wounded, many of the nursing personnel would have undoubtedly refused the order to take the first boats.

On deck, it was becoming obvious that delaying drill for the men until the next morning had been a serious error of judgement. Although there was no 'panic', no one knew what to do. To compound the difficulties and increase the casualty lists, the listing ship 'fouled the davits' and several lifeboats and their passengers were tipped into the sea. The accompanying Japanese destroyers rushed to *Transylvania*'s rescue. What Murphy called 'our second present from the Hun' – almost certainly directed towards the weaving and dodging Japanese rescuers, hit *Transylvania*. Doubly wounded she sank in under an hour, her captain going down with his vessel – his body was later washed ashore in Savona, Italy. Hundreds of men, including Williams, leapt from the sinking vessel on to the Japanese warship *Matsu* which had released its own lifeboats to make the 8–10ft jump marginally less hazardous. Williams remembered how *Matsu*'s crew, 'little fellows, very good at their job', offered the rescued personnel every kindness. Those found in the sea by Italian fishing vessels were equally well treated. Meanwhile *Sakaki* strove to protect the stricken *Transylvania* by keeping the U-boat submerged.

Murphy, meanwhile was in the sea, clinging to a life raft, no bigger than his mother's 'wicker card table' as he would do for some three hours. The initially calm sea became rougher and despite being 'continually thrown off my raft', he 'usually came up within easy reach of it' although three of the other officers clinging to it with him were not all so lucky. Eventually rescued by a fishing boat, he, like Williams, was taken to Savona. A devout Roman Catholic, he attributed his survival to the 'green scapulars which I had around my neck'. His family members were henceforth always made to travel wearing scapulars. Williams noted that the survivors were housed in a nearby army barracks although he was unimpressed by the black coffee served for breakfast and disconcerted by the Italian soldiers eating macaroni with their fingers. Both men attended the subsequent memorial and funeral service held on 6 May for *Transylvania*'s Captain and those who had perished, some of whose bodies were washed ashore: 'It was a sad moment' (Williams); the names of those lost are inscribed on the Savona Memorial to the Missing.

Also waiting in Marseille to board *Transylvania* was Norfolk-born TFNS Sister Jessie Clementia Hayward who had served at 1st Eastern General Hospital, Cambridge. In February 1917, the medical authorities considered her fit to 'undertake nursing duties in a military hospital abroad in an Eastern climate' and she was detailed for Salonica. Her port of departure would, like thousands of other troops destined for this theatre, be Marseille where she arrived at the nurses' camp on 2 May, undoubtedly the one that Sister Burgess found so un-conducive. At 4 am, excited but sad that the mail had not arrived, meaning she would have no last precious messages from home to accompany her on her first active posting overseas, Sister Hayward marched out of camp and by early afternoon had boarded *Transylvania*. Unlike Williams, she mentions a lifeboat drill taking place before supper, 'a farce as usual' and indeed a second 'private rehearsal' for the sisters, led by Matron, of the action to take should the vessel be torpedoed: 'We walk to our lifeboat. I am to be in charge of our corridor. Life belts always to be worn (some "grumble")'. Like Williams, she too waxed lyrical about the ship, 'lovely beautiful berths'. Sadly, Hayward would have but one night in which to enjoy her 'eiderdown [which] looks so nice.' Sunning themselves on deck in the early hours of the morning and chatting with the VADs, matron took the nursing personnel to task for failing to wear their life belts.

Within fifteen minutes of Matron's admonition, there was 'a bang which those who heard it will never forget'. Proving the benefit of the nursing personnel's 'private rehearsal', 'there is no panic, everyone goes to her allotted place'. Commenting on having heard the cry, 'Ladies First', Hayward's boat, containing '45 of us all pushed in, three Tommies', presumably to assist with rowing, is 'lowered. I really think this is the worst moment.' To the cheers of the men still on board (many of whom would have known from personal experience the inestimable value of professional nurses), the women set off in sea described by Hayward as 'rough'. With sisters also taking the oars, the shore did not initially seem too far away. Then, to her horror, she sees the second torpedo strike, now 'the waves are so big' and 'bailing out seems fruitless'. Then

> '*another bang and* Transylvania *is no more … The sea seems alive, men clinging to oars, rafts and boats, they look sadly at our boat and we are sinking … I and all the Sisters think we shall sink with the boat. I wonder what they will think at home.*

With waves now increasing in size, 'I am washed out and find myself clinging to an oar and a piece of rope.' Clinging quite literally for dear life to her oar and with arms aching beyond description, with waves crashing over her head and nauseous from all the seawater she was imbibing, she heard a voice saying that the Japanese destroyer was 'alongside'. Still retaining something of her sense of humour, or at least when she subsequently recounted the event, Hayward 'thought my head was going to be knocked and it was a pity to be killed after all the "holding on"'. Brandy, wine glugged out of the bottle, and a towel for warmth helped her to revive and 'bask in the relief of survival' and feel immeasurable gratitude towards the *Transylvania*'s Japanese rescuers.

With Savona in close sight, the rescued nurses were greeted and cheered by men who had already made it ashore from the stricken ship: 'What a reception we had. The Cheers! We felt quite heroines and had done nothing to deserve it… We must have looked weird, some wrapped in blankets, others in men's coats and all with wet draggled hair (I saved two hairpins only)'.

Maybe the Savona nuns who lodged the nurses in their nearby convent offered hairpins or perhaps this became the least of Sister Jessie Hayward's domestic worries as all personal kit naturally went down – along with Williams' Peerless lorries. Having also attended the funeral service for the dead and missing on 6 May, the Sisters who had returned to Marseille on 9 May were ordered to return to England to procure new kit.

Back in Marseille, the nurses started their return journey to England via Northern France. On board their Blighty-bound transport, Hayward noted: 'None of us slept very well and [we] clung to our life belts although the steward said they were not necessary!' With true British understatement she comments that should 'I ever get out to the East I hope it won't be so exciting as this' – or that at least that she had a suitable supply of hairpins. She arrived in Salonika on 9 September 1917; one can only imagine her fear as she again departed from Marseille. Demobilised in 1919, Queen Alexandra graciously allowed her to keep her TFNS badge as she had served for 'more than four years' as a Territorial Forces Nursing Sister.

Throughout the war, Marseille lived up to its long and troubled history. Its position was strategic, a maritime crossroads where men, women and matériel arrived and departed to feed the insatiable greed of total, mechanised warfare. Irrespective of its soldiers' bravery, its citizens' generosity, even of the *Marseillaise* itself, Marseille's reputation damned it in the eyes of many. Falsely accused by Parisian politicians of cowardly soldiers, its residents considered lazy by some and immoral by others, the city had proven itself ripe for gossip, discontent, intrigue and spies. But these self-same Marseillais had extended a warm and compassionate welcome to personnel from across the globe whose first sight of the country where they would lie forevermore was the port that traced its origins back to the sixth century BC.

Chapter 10

On the Loose No More

Amassing the evidence

Unbeknownst to those who would soon be suffering and dying on the infamous Chemin des Dames ridge, including countless men from Marseille, and to those who would perish on *Transylvania* as well as troops destined for Salonika, in Marseille the wheels of justice relating to a recently apprehended 'artiste lyrique' were turning. An 'Urgent' communication dated 14 March 1917 was sent to the Chief of Police of the 9ème Brigade de Police Mobile. He was to proceed to arrest the 'so-called Régina Diana in truth Avvico, Marie-Antoinette'. The initial surveillance operation would have been undertaken by gendarmes – for no other reason than they were a familiar sight and would have faded into the background as they 'policed' civilians as well as soldiers; the physical arrest however was entrusted to one of the crack Mobile Brigades which, formed during the Belle-Époque, had recently been responsible for arresting spies Mata Hari and Felice Pfaard. Nothing could be left to chance. Arrested on 16 March at her lodgings, 16 Rue Venture, when she was about to leave for the St Charles station, the Police Inspector reported that the suspect made no attempt to resist but advised him it would have been in better taste to apprehend her discreetly indoors rather than in a public place. As 16 Rue Venture was a hairdresser's establishment, an arrest outside the door would have been considered bad for business.

In Geneva, Mme Avvico was getting concerned. A neighbour later claimed that she had been overheard expressing alarm that she had heard nothing from her daughter who was normally such a reliable correspondent; she was becoming increasingly worried ('forte inquiète). Although the cameo of a mother's anxiety about her daughter puts a human face on the drama that was unfolding, this maternal concern would have been of little interest to the police. What interested them was whether Mme Avvico was privy to her daughter's espionage activities.

With Régina safely behind bars in the Maison de Correction for women, Les Présentines Marseille, the French authorities sought help from their Geneva consular staff and the Geneva police. They needed to amass as much evidence as possible to place before the gendarmes and subsequently a military tribunal. Between May and June 1917, a M. Monnet from the Geneva police assiduously gathered information relating to the domestic arrangements of 'la demoiselle Avvico' and her mother. He discovered that a 'gentleman from Zurich' (almost certainly the aforementioned 'LOUIS' and thus perhaps 'Aunt Louisa') regularly visited the Avvico apartment to collect information and hand over money. Having noted the friendship with Cherix whom he describes as a failed 'garagiste' and dealer in contraband rubber, Monnet reported the testimony of the Avvicos' neighbours at 7 Rue de Fribourg.

Then as now, this road was in a comfortable, quietly affluent part of Geneva, conveniently close to the station. The Avvico women's rapid rise in fortune which had enabled them to reside in an area that would not normally be within the financial reach of a former laundress and her chanteuse lyrique daughter, had not passed undetected. While the Swiss are known for their reticence, once questions were posed by the Geneva police about the activities of the mother and daughter, several neighbours were keen to share their unsympathetic feelings about the newcomers, stressing that the daughter particularly 'was up to no good'. The women whom Monnet interviewed were 'scandalised'. Although Régina had provided names of people who would testify in her defence, including her singing teacher, a Mlle. E. Chorange who may have helped to compose and subsequently teach her her 'signature' tune, 'Salut aux Alliés', all character referees' testimonies were dismissed by Monnet. He simply stated that all were known as ardent 'Germanophiles' – frustratingly, how he reached this conclusion is not stated. Not that he would have wished to bring this to the attention of his French counterparts, these sentiments were far from unusual in Geneva.

Whilst the Swiss were busy gathering information about this erstwhile Geneva resident, the aforementioned Dunand contacted a British General Intelligence Staff Officer Capt. P.J.G. Piper, asking him to shed light on the ships named in the confiscated postcards. It is worth pausing here to wonder whether simple postcards help provide the answer to why the U-boat campaign was so effective in the Mediterranean. Régina and others in her ring, including Févarotto, had been operational in the area over a significant period. In the understated words of the website *The Deadly Mediterranean*, 'From 1915–1917, U-boats ha[d] some stunning successes in the Mediterranean'. Many, although far from all, of these successes covered the precise time when Régina's ring was operational in the area. Testimony subsequently used against her at the trial (and the prosecution had no way of knowing what intelligence she had supplied to her German masters before the French closed in on her but it was undoubtedly significant), listed that she had sent information about: *Huntspill, Kashmir, Kalayan, Manitou* (unsuccessfully attacked in March 1917 en route to Alexandria as well as in May and in December 1917) and the ill-fated *Transylvania*. Postcards listing these ships were sent to Duchilio in Zurich. So sensitive was this information that Piper advised Dunand that, should he be called upon to testify, he could only refer to these vessels as numbers 1, 2, 3, 4 and 5.

On 30 August 1917 after a five-month long, in-depth inquiry which included over thirty-five interrogations of the accused, all conducted following the rulebook and meticulously transcribed by hand and initialled by 'M-A A', sufficient incriminating evidence had been amassed against her. Despite there being copious information, the feeling remains that this is the tip of a forever-submerged iceberg.

One must surmise that prospective agents would have undergone training in how to conduct themselves during an interrogation. Régina agrees with what she has written on the postcards but sticks to the story that these were the only ones that she sent. Here it is probable that her memory was highly selective. The amount of money she admits to regularly being paid (in excess of 1,000 Swiss (1,700 French) francs when Schragmüller's going rate was 400 Swiss francs for other than her most reliable agents); the luxurious hotel in which she entertained her lover[s] and the neighbourhood where her mother now resided, that when she was arrested her suitcase had already been taken to the station in advance by a 'commissionaire', would indicate someone at the peak of her game and consequently enjoying luxuries that would only have been offered to those whose supply of intelligence extended far beyond the unique four postcards she claimed to have sent. In short to an agent who had proved, quite literally, her worth. Her cover may have remained that of a singer and 'accompagnatrice', her undercover mission to lure men to their deaths, but in her financial status she had moved beyond the often seedy, impoverished café-concert world.

Weighing the evidence

The case was placed in front of the Conseil de Guerre of the XV ème Région d'Etat-Major – that self-same Région which, despite all its efforts and the heroic sacrifices of its soldiers, had never fully recovered from the calumny of August 1914. The court was convened on 17 September 1917. Perhaps surprisingly, at least to twenty-first century readers used to protracted cases, the trial did not even last three days and the minutes relating to the proceedings and judgement extend to a mere ten pages whilst the accumulated evidence comprises 470 other items.

Among these items a few pull at the heart strings and present the human face of a woman whom many would see simply as a ruthless agent. Nestling among the mountain of preserved papers are some of the letters that she had endeavoured to send to, as well as some she received from, her mother. Puzzlingly, Régina's letters are the originals. Had they been sent at all or were copies made and these sent to Geneva? While both women would have known that their correspondence would be scrutinised, no doubt in the attempt to gather more incriminating evidence, it is nevertheless hard not to be moved by the words exchanged a century ago between 'my dearest mother' and 'my beloved daughter', both adjuring the other to face the future with 'courage', feeling the letters narrowed the immense physical and emotional distance between them. As for the little girl in Crest, Régina asked her mother to tell her that she had had to go 'a long way away' but that the grandmother would provide news. In a letter dated 27 June 1917, Mme Avvico hoped that her granddaughter had been awarded good marks in her school examinations.

All that interested the prosecution was hard evidence. Yet one cannot help but wonder whether the speed of the trial was itself a form of what the French term 'justice expéditive' or summary justice, haste being essential to lance the poison festering in Marseille. Or was it just that the accumulated evidence was so overwhelming, why waste more of the military judges' time than was strictly necessary to demonstrate that justice had been done and Article 30 of the 1899 Hague Convention applied, namely that even when 'taken in the act [a spy] cannot be punished without previous trial'?

Undoubtedly one more nail in the coffin of Régina Diana, whom the court referred to by her legal name, Marie-Antoinette Avvico, was the testimony provided by a fellow inmate in Les Présentines. This woman had been planted to assist the prosecution in constructing their case against the accused, a ploy used by both sides and one which led to more than one spy, including Louise de Bettignies, incriminating themselves. This woman whose name was struck from the minutes of the proceedings, either to avoid retaliation or preserve her usefulness should she be needed in the future, stated that during a period of several weeks, the accused had repetitively used unpatriotic language, being more than disdainful in her speech towards the soldiers fighting for France. Furthermore, she had, on countless occasions, insulted the Republic by using 'crude language and gestures' in the process. It is tempting to see Régina's background as a café-concert artiste coming to the fore here. To ensure that the French sung their way to Victory in an appropriate manner, songs were frequently accompanied by gestures. The witness added that her cellmate had clearly despised France and claimed that if she had had the possibility and opportunity she would have destroyed the country herself. This is in direct contrast to what Régina told her interrogators, namely that she had never harboured ill feeling towards France and penury alone had thrust her into the world of espionage.

In modern legal language, this plant's evidence would have been labelled 'hearsay', but in a 1917 spy trial it was admissible. Furthermore, this was an era when public opinion was largely shaped by what people were told to do, say, and believe, and as many French historians including the eminent Stéphane Audoin-Rouzeau have pointed out, the French like all other populations, had been subject to intensive brainwashing or 'bourrage du crâne' since the opening days of hostilities. Relatively few members of the public, had they heard this testimony, nor indeed those seven military men sitting in judgement who had no legal background, would have paused to reflect upon its provenance or its reliability. But, as far as the public was concerned, none would have heard because the hall in which the trial was conducted had had to be evacuated and the session adjourned, then simply cancelled. On 20 September 1917, the President of the Court pronounced the guilty verdict and the sentence at one and the same time. In accordance with Article 81 of the Military Code, the civilian, Marie-Antoinette Avvico alias Régina Diana, was to be executed by firing squad.

The process of law was not yet complete – justice still had both to be done and to be seen to be done, and the legality of the case and the court findings confirmed. Should clemency be extended or was the case solid and should the relevant article of the Military Code be enforced? For Marie-Antoinette and her mother (and no doubt also for those who had found her guilty), a nail-biting two months followed. The judgement was dispatched to the Military Court ('Conseil de Révision') in Lyon. The findings and sentence were duly approved on 22 October 1917. Now it was for the Court of Appeal ('Cour de Cassation') in Paris to reach a final decision which it did on 22 November 1917.

Chapter 11

The Spy-catcher's Manual

'Half military half civilian': Gendarme spy catchers

Throughout the war, Swiss citizens' interest in spying remained high: plays, serialised stories and news reports kept their appetites whetted as did the occasional account of an execution. The 4 October 1917 *Gazette de Lausanne* reported an 'invitation' issued by the French War Ministry to all public prosecutors to increase the 'zeal' with which they apprehended spies and to be particularly vigilant for citizens of neutral states potentially operating in France on Germany's behalf. The paper's correspondent may have been unaware that a Geneva resident had, in the fortnight preceding the article, faced a military tribunal in Marseille on charges of espionage. The verdict had just been handed down, although not yet confirmed.

In order to try to protect the Confederation's neutral status, before as well as during the First World War, the government had passed numerous laws relating to spies detained on Swiss territory. Military courts could impose high monetary fines, and call for lengthy terms of imprisonment. Despite heavy penalties being available to the courts, reading through press accounts of trials and verdicts in the work of *inter alia* Christophe Vuilleumier, it is soon apparent that even those caught red-handed, or whose guilt was proven beyond all reasonable doubt, generally escaped with a negligible fine and a suspended prison sentence. Women were treated even more lightly than men. Perhaps these trials instilled a false sense of security in those who, at the behest of German handlers, made their way to and from neutral Switzerland to spy in France.

If penalties handed down in Switzerland to those who were found guilty of spying were often derisory, for spies caught in France, the stakes were immeasurably higher. Laws 204–208 of the French military penal code made provision for the death sentence to be passed on those caught spying in time of war. But for this sentence to be passed, due process of law had to be observed and the French had checks and balances in place to ensure that all who were involved in the deadly game knew their role and how to perform it.

The story of those who played a part in apprehending spies and bringing them to trial is little known but can be pieced together using Régina's papers and research undertaken by a historian of the Gendarmerie Nationale.

Spycatchers were working in a frenzied atmosphere for spy fever had gripped Europe in the late nineteenth and very early twentieth century; the French popular press served up a diet of melodramatic articles. To name just two, the satirical weekly *L'Assiette au Beurre* devoted the whole of its 2 October 1909 edition to lurid spy stories and in 1910, Paul Lanoir's *L'Espionnage Allemand en France: Son Organisation – Ses Dangers – Les Remèdes Nécessaires* (translated and available in Britain as *The German Spy System in France)* aimed to alert Frenchmen to the dangers they faced from German espionage. It was rapidly re-issued after war had broken out.

If the reading public were being stirred up into a frenzy of anxiety about potential (invariably German) enemy agents, from the beginning of the twentieth century, the French Sûreté Générale (SG) had become increasingly involved in national security and intelligence work, one of its main aims being the pursuit of enemy agents in France. During the war, the SG claimed to have arrested some 3,200 individuals suspected of espionage; not all cases proceeded to trial and only a percentage were executed. In May 1915, to strengthen national security, Alexandre Millerand had created the Section de Centralisation du Renseignement (SCR) under the command of Captain Georges Ladoux; its express mission was to oversee the work of civilian and military counterintelligence in France.

Both these secret service organisations worked hand-in-glove with the Gendarmerie created in 1791. Its First World War history still under-researched, the Gendarmerie was (and still is) part of the French Army. Yet, under the jurisdiction of both the French War and Home Offices, it is, in Napoleon Bonaparte's words quoted by Jen-Noel Luc, 'half military, half civilian'. Regular soldiers who were often considerably older than combatants, gendarmes' role in the war was far wider than that of the British Military Police. They were almost always responsible for arresting spies both at the Front and in the rear and, from the earliest days, it was impressed upon them that along with matters pertaining to military discipline, this would be one of their key roles. Desperately unpopular with soldiers at the Front but often appreciated by civilians in the rear, gendarmes both during and after the war were keen to be seen and remembered as spy catchers standing between France and enemy infiltration.

French gendarme and historian Louis Panel has researched many aspects of this force and its involvement with counterespionage during the war. In his redacted PhD thesis which formed the basis of his article 'Espionnage et trahison …', his findings allow us to understand the arrest, interrogation and conduct of Régina and other spies' trials, thereby putting the human face on the court papers.

As early as November 1914, the duties of gendarmes brought them into close contact with their Swiss counterparts through keeping a watchful eye on border traffic including individuals crossing between France and neutral countries, particularly Switzerland. Alexandre Millerand felt that these were the areas where France was most vulnerable to infiltration. Anyone who even appeared to be suspect should be detained as soon as they had crossed into France and lengthy checks undertaken regarding their credentials. Either the spies were too clever or the gendarmes insufficiently vigilant as, despite the minister's exhortations, spies continued to cross the borders into France even in late 1918. People who had legitimate contacts on both sides of the Franco-Swiss borders were particularly valuable to spymasters and, conversely, became of especial interest to those undertaking surveillance operations.

The French site Mémoire des Hommes records a total of 126 spies executed by France during the war; nine (seven per cent) of whom were women, despite, according to Panel, seventy per cent of the list of suspects drawn up by the French security services being female. He believes that this imbalance is explained by 'Conseils de Guerre' (military courts) being reluctant to pass the death sentence on women; they would only have done so in the 'gravest cases', which Régina's undoubtedly was.

To help them function both efficiently and in a uniform manner across France, gendarmes were provided with what can best be described as a manual ('carnet)' which they had to carry at all times. This outlined the correct procedures to be followed when closing in on suspects in both militarised and non-militarised areas including railway stations – it was felt that the rail network would be the preferred method of infiltration for most spies. Gendarmes regularly patrolled trains checking on soldiers and *permissionnaires*; they were advised to scrutinise any passenger whose papers did not appear to be in perfect order and whose identity and nationality could not be instantly established. Those whom they considered suspicious were to be disembarked at the next station and taken to the nearest police station or gendarmerie. There is ample evidence in her trial papers that Régina frequently travelled by train, indeed she was on her way to Marseille station when she was arrested. One wonders whether her heart missed a beat every time she was approached by a gendarme, particularly as they had been told to be vigilant of foreigners who made multiple train journeys; the manual stipulated that people should have solid reasons for their journey. It would appear from her documents however, that her papers and passport had the correct visas, all her comings and goings meticulously recorded with multiple official stamps. On the surface, she may have felt that she had little to fear; after all, as she stressed during interrogation, she was the daughter of a Frenchwoman, resident of neutral Switzerland and citizen of France's Ally, Italy.

Although Panel states that the gendarmes' manual exhorted them to be especially vigilant in railway stations, it is probable that they were also warned about the vulnerability of major ports. Spymasters such as Elisabeth Schragmüller were interested in shipping; Régina's copious information about the ships that she had seen at anchor in Marseille, including numbers of men presumed to be boarding them, formed part of the damning evidence against her. Although contemporary authors such as Basil Thomson noted disparagingly that 'lacking in technical knowledge … women misunderstand what they hear', Régina accurately noted the names of ships and, with one exception, regiments which were embarking. As early as May 1915, concerned that too many spies and other undesirables were slipping through the gendarmes' net, the force was told to increase its vigilance, to extend this well beyond stations, carry out careful checks of all hotels and be more aware of the provenance of visitors, especially foreign ones and ascertain the reasons for their presence. Here Régina's cover as a 'chanteuse lyrique' was watertight.

Another of the gendarmes' duties which has direct relevance to Régina's case is their responsibility to prevent letters circulating that could have divulged strategically important information. Régina's letters would have been routinely scrutinised because, as early as 9 July 1915, senior gendarme officer Major-General Pellé had informed his men that all letters between France and Switzerland were to be opened. Not only were they to check for military information, they were also advised to prevent letters circulating that hinted at civilian morale, highly significant in times of war; the trial papers make it clear that Régina was under express orders to report on prices, strikes (which by 1917 were paralysing Marseille, like many other parts of France) and inflation. These were the precise details that interested Schragmüller who had long realised that protracted wars are not won on the battlefield alone. Many of the envelopes addressed to Switzerland in Régina's file bear evidence that they had been opened and the overt content read by the authorities – it was standard practice to stamp letters to say that they had been opened under military orders. Aware of the proliferation of the use of invisible ink, its sale was banned; those who, like Régina, contravened this order could, if caught, anticipate the full force of the law descending upon them, even a charge of espionage.

If letters are easily opened and read, gendarmes were advised to be discreet in their physical surveillance of suspects. Drawing attention to themselves would alert the prey before they were ready to spring the trap. The manual provided gendarmes with helpful guidelines concerning to whom they should pay careful attention – once again Régina ticks many of the boxes. She held an Italian passport and 'foreigners', even nationals of Allied countries, were considered more suspect than French citizens as were those from (especially francophone) neutral states who would easily blend in with the local population and not attract attention to themselves. Individuals with what was termed a 'nomadic' way of life were to be watched; music hall artistes often fell into this category as many would have only been engaged for a few performances at any one venue. Furthermore, women who were seen associating with soldiers or men on leave who were not family members automatically came under suspicion. Panel noted that prostitutes – some of whom were also music hall artistes, were always in the gendarmes' sights, not only out of concern for the spreading of 'disease' amongst soldiers and sailors on leave but for fear that they may be spies.

Once attention had centred upon a person, reports would have been diffused, possibly by cable, to the various agencies and gendarmes responsible for counter-espionage. Along with a 'usable' physical description, precise data would have included reasons why the person had attracted attention. Gendarmes were reminded that whatever their suspicions, the work they were carrying out was delicate and had to comply with the 1886 law which stipulated that the case against potential spies had to be robust and, although they may follow someone on a hunch, evidence had to be solid and stand up to legal scrutiny. Any researcher who has scrutinised the various files on the *Mémoire des Hommes* website can attest to the amount of detailed information amassed against those who were tried. Every shred of evidence was documented, photographed and reproduced, leading contemporary gendarme instructor Albert Michel to admit that this led to a mountain of paperwork ('une paperasse démentielle') – to which he appears to have been more than willing to contribute.

A Practical Guide to Spy Catching and Interrogation

Article 30 of the 1899 Hague Conventions, to which France was a signatory, stipulated that a spy could not be punished without having been tried. Trial is of course, a necessary step along the path towards sentencing. When the spy is finally detained, rules need to be stringently followed.

In 1919, Albert Michel published a manual of *Matters to be taught to trainee gendarmes*. Written with the express aim of 're-francising' gendarmes in Alsace and Lorraine, this gives valuable additional insight into how interrogations were conducted and takes us to the final dénouement of Régina's story.

Michel explains to recruits that every step in the dance between suspect and interrogator had to be minutely choreographed. Thus a century later we may not have photographic evidence to tell us about the room in which Régina found herself but, thanks to Michel, we know that it would have been 'neither too hot nor too cold', that while her interrogators' faces (two interrogators were considered better than one in more complex cases) would be in semi-shadow, she would be seated (should she wish to sit) in such a way that her face was fully lit so that not even the tiniest fleeting expression was lost on those watching her. Indeed, in cases considered of extreme importance an observer, hidden to the suspect, monitored and subsequently commented upon almost every blink of their eye. Again, thanks to Michel's manual, we know the interrogator's attitude towards Régina would have been 'meticulously correct' throughout, although he would have needed to be, and appear to be, in control of the situation as it developed. 'Correct' behaviour was not restricted to the interrogation process; Michel stresses that those who approached civilians with a view to apprehending them should avoid any comportment that could be considered brusque, brutal or provocative, and the same courtesy should be extended to all, irrespective of their social status.

Gendarmes were advised that interrogations should not go on so long as to render the detainee tired; he or she had to be in full possession of their faculties ('en possession de leurs facultés') throughout the proceedings. Perhaps concerns for levels of fatigue extended beyond the suspect and included those who were transcribing the interview. As Michel noted and French files relating to wartime spies bear witness, court proceedings were written out by hand – in Régina's case, these extend to many closely written pages, frustratingly, not assembled in any obvious order. Nevertheless, it is possible, one hundred years later, to follow the trial as it unfolded and feel some sympathy for the transcriber. The manuscript relating to the interrogation was of crucial importance as this would be circulated to all the necessary authorities who would decide if the evidence were sufficient to warrant prosecution according to Article 597 of the 'Code Militaire'. It would also form the basis of the judgement.

Once evidence had been accumulated and interrogations concluded, the handwritten details were handed over to the army who could either proceed to trial or dismiss the case. The gendarmes had little further official part to play in either the trial or the sentencing although no doubt those who had been involved would have been interested to learn the verdict. In *La Grande Guerre des Gendarmes*, Panel argues that irrespective of the myth portrayed in contemporary popular literature and trench journals, gendarmes did not participate in firing squads (even for those sentenced at the Front), although they were present for public order duties at executions and, at least in the case of Mata Hari, a gendarme handcuffed her to the execution post.

With the gendarmes having done much of the preliminary evidence-gathering, Régina's trial was held in September 1917 in Marseille, headquarters of the XVème Corps or Region; each French Army Corps' headquarters had a permanent 'Conseil de Guerre' or 'War Council' to which espionage cases, as well as military matters pertaining to their area, were brought. Depending upon the gravity of the charges, up to six officers would act as judges; like their British counterparts, none had to be legally trained. Should the accused be from lower social classes, provision was made for an additional NCO to be on the panel of judges, in Régina's case, Sergeant Petit of the 141ème RI. Her hearing was conducted under the authority of Lieutenant Colonel Kervello, President of the Marseille Conseil de Guerre. One can only speculate as to whether those called upon to try her dreaded new calumny descending upon Marseille if the case were reported in the national press. All military trials could be public but should he feel that this was in the national interest, the court recorder could ban news reports. After Régina's public arraignment by Kervello, the courtroom was emptied of spectators, possibly because the material was considered sensitive.

From the outset, the accused was provided with the services of a lawyer. Perhaps to deflect any public opprobrium that they may be defending enemies of the nation, some claimed that they were acting purely out of a love of justice. Many were, according to Panel, at the peak of their profession; he believes some were titillated by the prospect of media attention, as in the case of Mata Hari. Counter to some of her biographers, he argues that Hari was 'brilliantly defended' although not, one might add, brilliantly enough to exonerate her. The first lawyer whom Régina approached, Mouton de Guérin, was, as she explained to the court reporter ('rapporteur') Lieutenant Dunand, unwilling to take the case. She had copious correspondence with Dunand pertaining to many matters but, frustratingly, his responses do not form part of the dossier, although at one point she bewails the fact that he has not replied to a query. The reasons for Guérin's rejection were not given in his terse response; maybe he saw her case as unwinnable. He referred it to a colleague, Maître Jean Grisoli who accepted and advised her to throw herself on the court's mercy. Lawyers often sought to delay the case coming to court for as long as possible as a guilty verdict and the death penalty were the likely outcomes. Defendants had to pay for their defence and at one point she seeks Dunand's permission to sell some jewellery held in the prison vaults in order to settle her legal costs; there were still 400 francs outstanding of the submitted bill of 1,000 francs. She would also need to cover the cost of the trial, some thirty plus francs (a litre of milk cost one franc in 1917).

Spy cases involving foreign nationals could have international ramifications, the authorities were keen to demonstrate that everything was above board; official recorders transcribed every word uttered. Once the evidence had been submitted the court retired to deliberate on whether the detainee were guilty of the crime of which he or she was accused and whether there were any extenuating circumstances. The verdict having been reached, all judges signed the final judgement papers. Press reporters meanwhile rushed to file their stories. In Régina's case, news of the court's conclusions was announced in several Paris papers, with the drama, which had not yet reached its final act, being picked up not only in London but also in distant Australia as well as, fittingly, in Algiers.

In wartime France, the final decision on those duly condemned to death by a court martial rested with the President of the Republic whose pronouncement was, in all cases, final; all papers pertaining to those upon whom the death penalty had been pronounced had to be submitted to this highest authority in the land via the Cour de Cassation. This gave those condemned under military law the right to appeal to a civilian or political authority – a right which Régina, like most if not all other spies, exercised. Might she perhaps have hoped that the Swiss would intervene on her behalf as they had occasionally successfully done on behalf of their nationals? The President had the power to exercise total clemency, to commute sentences to life imprisonment with or without hard labour, or ensure that the condemned man or woman began their last, frequently public, journey to the stake with the stirring words of the song of 'Le Régiment de Meuse et de Sambre' ringing, ironically, in their ears.

What of Régina's appeal? In the opinion of the 'Cour de Cassation', the prosecution had proved its case and the appeal was consequently rejected. No further avenue for either appeal or clemency existed. 'Ordres Particuliers No. 164' confirmed the telegramme 'Ministériel no 00484 2/10' dated 4

January. The President of the Republic, Raymond Poincaré, 'had decided justice should take its course', and instructed the dread sentence be carried out on Saturday 5 January 1918 at 6.30am at the 'Champ de Tir PHARO'. Then, in a moment of near-bathos, human error slips in. The typist had forgotten that the year had changed and dated this final communiqué 'le 4 Janvier 1917'.

No evidence remains whether at any point an attempt was made to negotiate a deal with Régina – or has this been expunged from the records? Might the authorities not have wished to discover or confirm the names of her contacts, the names of her German bosses? It was only after the war that the French Service de Renseignements seems to have become aware of the existence of Elisabeth Schragmüller. Or were *Abteilung IIIb*'s spies so well trained that most went to their graves with their lips sealed? Such was either Régina's secrecy or the French authorities' lack of questioning that she, like Louise de Bettignines, took with her to her grave the complete list of all the members of her ring.

The Final Act: 'Aim for the heart, men!'

Panel notes that although the press could be banned from the courtroom, they flocked, along with members of the public, to the site of the execution which in Paris was the Chateau de Vincennes and in Marseille le 'Champ de Tir du Pharo'. He argues that by allowing, perhaps even encouraging, the press and the public to attend spy executions, the authorities provided 'cathartic release' for a nation in mourning. The condemned individual served as a convenient conduit for both the grief and anger that had long simmered near the surface in France. Furthermore, seeing a spy shot could act as a useful deterrent – a point also made in previous centuries about public executions. While some citizens attended out of 'morbid curiosity', others were driven by the desire to jeer at those who had been caught hand-in-glove with the much-loathed Boches. Did any feel a grain of sympathy for the blindfold spy as he or she fell to the ground or did the crowd simply disperse, feeling that justice had been done and that the gendarmes, the Brigade de Police Mobile, and the military court had admirably completed the tasks assigned to them by the Sûreté Générale?

Spectators who, at 6.30 am on 5 January 1918 had flocked to witness this final act in Régina's life story would have assembled behind the firing party. As the courtroom had been emptied during the trial, some may have been eager to see justice meted out to the woman who had risked reopening barely healed wounds and brought further calumny upon their city, giving those living closer to the killing fields of northern and eastern France an opportunity to traduce Marseille for once again being derelict in her duty by allowing this spy to flourish in their midst.

Handcuffed to the execution post, weakened by weeks of imprisonment, Marie-Antoinette would certainly have shivered as the freezing breeze from the sea whistled through the pine trees, embracing this end of the Champ de Tir; gulls would have circled overhead. Did she shudder as the twenty-five-man firing squad readied and steadied itself, rifles at rest against their right thigh? Out of the corner of her eye she might have glimpsed the 20-year-old Lieutenant Mandal of the 3éme Régiment d'Infanterie Coloniale march up to his platoon and, in a swift movement, release the blade of his ordonnance sword from its scabbard and bark the order. 'Load!' Could she hear the metal clicking as each magazine delivered the cartridge into the chamber? The muzzles of twenty-five rifles would have been raised to shoulder height as the commander bellowed 'Take aim!' The command 'Fire' would have quickly followed.

Executions and their aftermath follow a well-established order and once the shots had been fired, the Chief Medical Officer of the Northern Barracks of Marseille would have moved solemnly forward. Doubtless all eyes would have been upon him as he bent over the bullet-riddled woman, revolver at the ready to administer, if needs be, the final *coup de grace*, before pronouncing her dead. Now the body could be removed.

The official proclamation made, the undertaker performed the next step in this carefully arranged drama. With the corpse placed in a makeshift coffin placed on a wagon drawn by a single horse, the earthly remains of just one more victim of a brutal war would have begun their final journey. Yet a feeling of unease remained nonetheless. Hardened as he was by dealing with those executed by firing squad during this brutal and brutalising war, the undertaker had never hitherto heard the order, '*Messieurs! Visez le Cœur! La cible est petite mais visez le cœur*' ('Men! Aim for the heart! It's a small target but aim for it'.)

And why, the undertaker might have wondered, a twenty-five-man squad; not the usual six to eight (occasionally twelve) deployed on a regular basis? As the archived documents specify, every rifle was loaded with a live round as opposed to alternating with a blank cartridge. This thirty-two-year old woman was guilty of such a terrible crime that the military wanted to ensure that under no circumstances, could she survive. Of the twenty-five rounds, twelve impacted on the body, three directly hitting the heart. Justice had been meted out. Something else that might have played on the undertaker's mind when looking at the still figure now lying on the slab in his preparation room, was that she was not wearing the regular blindfold most prisoners wore at the time the sentence was carried out. Reputedly, she, like the Belgian spy Gabrielle Petit executed by the Germans in Brussels on 1 April 1916, had preferred to look death and her executioners in the eye.

In wartime, even execution has its rituals, including a clear division between military and civilian offences. During the war, those condemned to death for high treason were either shot or hanged: shot if the perpetrator fell under military jurisdiction, hanged if civilian. In France, additional suffering was meted out to the relatives and family of those who had paid with their life for their crime: they could not bury the deceased nor even attend the funeral ceremony. This, so the authorities imagined, prevented any graveside diatribe against France and the Union Sacrée. The body was disposed of in a common burial pit in an unknown location, denied even the dignity of a headstone. In contrast, the British authorities, having executed eleven spies in the Tower of London, took them for burial at the East London Cemetery in Plaistow, where they remain to this day; some with elaborate headstones, others with simple grave markers.

In even greater contrast was the grief, collective mourning and ultimately adulation heaped upon those who had had the good fortune to spy for the winning side and whose bodies, like those of Edith Cavell, Gabrielle Petit and Louise de Bettignies, were exhumed and re-buried, with the monuments erected to them becoming sites of national, at times international, pilgrimage. Those executed in France for espionage were literally erased from the surface of the earth, the very existence of their temporal remains denied, their next of kin deprived of any inheritance and even presented with a bill for both the trial and expenses incurred gathering evidence – and also the bullets used.

A nameless, unidentifiable common burial pit remains the final resting place of this highly colourful, loud and enigmatic woman. Was she, one is forced to wonder, a helpless pawn caught up in a game that was too intricate and too complicated, whose rules she did not fully comprehend or was she, like spymistress Elisabeth Schragmüller, glorying in her power? She knew that the stakes were high but they would enable her to prove her worth, her value and maybe permanently move away from the life of a café-concert and music hall artiste, forced at times to supplement her income by prostitution; ever at the beck and call, and sometimes in the bed, of the director of whichever establishment in which she was performing.

Perhaps those who read about the execution, be it in the Swiss, French, Australian or British press, might have paused to wonder why a woman in her early thirties had met this gruesome end in a far-flung corner of Marseille's quartier Nord. Régina's execution was, as far as Anglo and francophone readers were concerned, of a woman working for the 'enemy', putting her beyond the pale of compassion for almost, if not all, of those who read the news. Even those who, in earlier years, might have felt disturbed by the execution of a woman, might now have been hardened by the horrors of the bloodshed and carnage of three and a half long years of war. Both sides were united in passing the death sentence on any spy upon whom they could lay their hands. Spies, be they male or female, still considered by many to be among the lowest of the low, could expect to receive no quarter, no public mercy and little private compassion.

Did any readers or spectators pause to wonder precisely what steps the condemned woman had taken which had led to this lonely death before dawn broke on 5 January 1918? Did any ask who precisely was Marie-Antoinette Avvico, alias 'Régina Diana' who had developed, organised, and created a network which, at the peak of its glory, stretched from Germany to France and from France to Algeria, with Switzerland and Italy as rear bases? Given the strictures of the time in which she was working, her achievements are breath-taking, even more so when we remember that she was a simple milliner-cum café-concert artiste from lowly beginnings in Geneva.

Singer, Siren, Spy

Régina was part of a system, in some ways, little more than a pawn in a complex game of chess with the moves orchestrated by minds far greater than her own. To use modern terminology, handlers on both sides saw spies who were arrested and subsequently sentenced to death or life imprisonment as 'collateral damage'. Like their British and French counterparts, there was nothing they could or would do to assist them, even assuming they knew that they had been rumbled.

How quickly the news of Régina's disappearance reached her German masters and other interested parties we will never know. Did the 'gentleman from Zurich' who had visited her mother raise alarm bells or even report on her imprisonment, and was her demise anticipated? Once the normal routine of postcards to Switzerland was interrupted, Zurich would have known it was only a matter of time before the French arrested her. Did anyone in that Swiss German 'nest of spies' comb the newspapers and maybe read in *Le Matin* (Paris) of 24 November 1917 that final judgement had been pronounced on 'Mme Avvico dite Régina Diana'? This Parisian paper had again been quick to report this latest scandal originating in Marseille, that city in the sun-kissed South whose 'aimable' soldiers had, or so the paper claimed, once brought dishonour on French arms. It appears to have been the first to carry the news that the Appeal Court had rejected the appeal for clemency. The ultra-Catholic newspaper *La Croix* (Paris) hoped to reassure its readers on 28 November 1917 that the guilty party was German which, had they read this, may have led to a cynical raising of eyebrows among her recent handlers. Schragmüller would almost certainly have bewailed the loss of 2,000 francs – the fine which *La Croix* reported, had been imposed by the court. The 12 January 1918 edition of the *Journal de Genève* tucked on an inside page the news that the ultimate act in the drama had been achieved. A former resident of Geneva, an Italian artiste Marie-Antoinette Avvico, whose signature tune and music-hall sketch, 'Salut aux Alliés' had been specially composed by Geneva lyricists for her to sing in Marseille, had been shot by firing squad. She would lure men to their deaths no more. And, to complete this tour of the francophone press, across the Mediterranean in Algiers, had anyone noticed in the 22 September 1917 *Echo d'Algiers*, one of the first newspapers to report the story, that the woman one of their officers had considered 'so lovable' had been found guilty of espionage?

French Prime Minister Georges Clemenceau was among the many men who claimed that 'Women cannot do much damage for they do not understand warfare'. In this case, as in that of so many female spies throughout history whose stories have been either alluded to or briefly revealed in this book, had the authorities been less complacent about women's ability to acquire and understand military information, they may have closed in more quickly on Marie-Antoinette Avvico alias Régina Diana who, like all combatants and intelligence agents on both sides during this so-called Great War, had blood on her hands. She, as well as being a singer, was also both a siren and a spy.

Chapter 12

A Post-bellum Post Script

While Régina's fate was sealed at Marseille's firing range at 6:30am on 5 January 1918, returning her to the obscurity from which she had briefly emerged, the lives and memories of others who appear in this book stretched into the post-bellum world.

Louise de Bettignies

Post-war, the vanquished could do little to honour the achievements of their own intelligence agents; however, to the victor the spoils and the winning side took pains to commemorate many of those who had spied on their behalf. None more so than Louise de Bettignies. On 21 February 1920, a coffin bearing her exhumed body was placed on a gun carriage and, with the French and British Armies providing full military honours, she was repatriated and buried with her family at St Amand aux Eaux, near Lille. On 13 November 1927, Maréchal Foch presided over the unveiling of a monument to Louise de Bettignies. Few if any of those attending the ceremony honouring this brave and dedicated agent would have spared a thought for those soldiers sent to their graves by her actions. She was, and rightly remains, revered as the most heroic of the 'heroic women of the Occupied Territories'.

Switzerland and Ulrich Wille

By November 1918, spies and their threat to Swiss neutrality had faded into the background. It is doubtful if, ten months later, anyone remembered reading about erstwhile Geneva resident Marie-Antoinette Avvico alias Régina Diana; the country was facing unprecedented political upheaval. The eye-watering rise of around 195 per cent in the cost of living, the approximate six per cent drop in workers' wages, and the lack of political and labour rights were sources of mounting tension. Although there had been spasmodic strikes throughout the war, events were reaching a climax; rebellion was in the air.

At the very moment when the Entente Cordiale countries celebrated the Armistice and the Central Powers swallowed the bitter pill of defeat, the

Swiss Army was keeping order in two key Swiss cities. Although not the first time that soldiers had been used to quell wartime labour unrest, disturbances had been low-key. On this occasion, two infantry regiments and two cavalry brigades from Luzern and Thurgau (so-called 'safe' rural areas of Switzerland) comprising some 95,000 troops had been sent to occupy the cities of Zurich and Berne; heavy machine guns were emplaced near Zurich station; a volatile situation was being rapidly inflamed. Accusing the government of seeking to establish a military dictatorship, labour leaders called a general strike – but using good Swiss common sense, only on a Saturday (9 November), thereby losing half, as opposed to a full day's, labour. The following day, defying government orders, celebrations marked the first anniversary of the Russian Revolution. Troops dispersed the illegal revellers leaving one dead and several wounded. Fearful of a looming civil war, on 14 November, both sides took a step back. General Ulrich Wille saw this as a vindication of the use of a strong military presence, others, as further indication of his intimidation strategy. The Swiss Historical Dictionary places the initial responsibility for sending in the troops on Wille, other historians place this on the Federal Assembly encouraged by Wille.

Irrespective of which source is the more accurate, General of Switzerland Ulrich Wille's post-bellum career was not the one he might have anticipated had the vision he shared in his letters to his wife Clara of England's defeat (1 February 1917) and international recognition of the 'greatness of Germany' (20 February 1917) materialised. When Wille retired on 11 December 1918, his dream of German hegemony in tatters, the Federal Assembly politely expressed the country's gratitude for his service but was less than effusive in its praise of his four years' (rather lacklustre) achievements.

Spymasters in Chief: Walter Nicolaï and Fraulein Doktor

In early 1919 Walter Nicolaï was reported to be 'on gardening leave', he was formally retired on 20 February 1920. However, an Irish Brigade internet source suggests that owing to his knowledge of Russian, between 1921 and 1924 he was *Gruppenleite of Sondergruppe R (Russland)* (Head of Special Intelligence [Russia]) and that he subsequently established the Republic of Turkey's first intelligence organisation.

Believing that many accounts of Germany's intelligence operations both during and after the war were sensationalised, Markus Pöhlmann argues that Nicolaï's post-war life was 'unspectacular'. Not only was he largely excluded from the re-building of Germany's intelligence services in the new Weimar

Republic, he was also excluded from contributing to the official history of *Abteilung III(b)*. In 1944, 71-year-old Nicolaï left war-shattered Berlin for supposedly safer quarters in Nordhausen. Such safety proved illusory. In early July 1945, he was arrested at his home by the occupying Soviet troops, his papers seized and taken to Moscow as war booty. Like thousands of others from the area, he was deported to Russia and interrogated by the Russian Secret Police. He died in May 1947 in a Moscow hospital within the prison compound which was his final home. He was buried in a mass grave. In 1999, the Russian Military Public Prosecutor posthumously exonerated him and made his papers available – although they have attracted little interest. In terms of the elusive Fraulein Doktor, those who have examined this archive confirm that the documents corroborate information about Nicolaï's most gifted recruit whose undertakings impacted so significantly upon events in Switzerland and, by extension, upon Régina's story.

As far as Nicolaï was concerned, he considered no praise was too high for this exceptional woman whom he had, in the very first instance, been reluctant to include in his network. Despite significant efforts and appeals made to both Erich Ludendorff and General Erich von Falkenhayn, Nicolaï failed to acquire the Iron Cross for this most 'outstanding personality', nor, contrary to popular opinion including some internet sources, was she ever given officer rank in the German Army. His words in *Geheime Mächte: Internationale Spionage und ihre Bekämpfung im Weltkrieg und heute* (Leipzig: K. F. Koehler, 1924 p. 174) are the perfect summation of her achievements:

> *Agents are a folk shimmering in all colours and they require above all guidance by an outstanding personality. The ability to judge a character and to think straight, and sophistication in personal interaction with people are indispensable as well. It is significant that in the German intelligence service … an extraordinary well educated woman knew best about handling agents, even the most difficult and sly ones.*

Post war, Dr Elisabeth Schragmüller took up a university post but, as a woman, her work never received full recognition. Leni Riefenstahl's proposed 1933 biopic fell victim to the ban on all German-made spy films; the 1937 French film *Mademoiselle Docteur* is far more fiction than fact. In 1934, her SA [Brown shirt] brother Johann Konrad was assassinated following the Night of the Long Knives. Despite sensational stories, there is nothing to indicate that she was involved with either the Nazi party or its wartime intelligence although Nicolaï believed that her early death prevented her from being recalled to service. All that is known for certain is that suffering from bone tuberculosis, Dr Elisabeth Schragmüller died in obscurity on 24 February 1940, her grave in Bad Tolz lost, her contribution to her beloved Fatherland's intelligence service all but forgotten.

Marseille, 'Marraine de Guerre'

In late 1914 when Jean Faber developed the godmother or 'marraine de guerre' idea, he suggested that towns and cities far from the Front 'adopt' those suffering from the physical effects of the war and contribute to their re-building. On 22 February 1915, the committee 'La Provence pour le Nord' was inaugurated. Provençal newspapers, company directors and individuals of all classes and monetary means from the maligned 'amiable South' saw this as a concrete way of demonstrating that as well as sacrificing her sons, Marseille was cognisant of the agony of towns on the front line. Two weeks later, a charitable fund was established; Marseillais flocked to contribute both hundreds of francs and the widow's mite. Within six months the fund stood at some 300,000 francs and money flowed in throughout the war. One widow went as far as to proclaim that her donation was a response to the injustices heaped upon Marseille and Provence.

With peace on the horizon, in October 1918, the committee announced that ravaged Arras would henceforth be Marseille's 'godchild'. With his city and its historic buildings almost obliterated from four long years of being on, and at times in front of, the front line, the elderly, war-weary mayor of Arras could barely contain his joy when his counterpart from Marseille officially visited his residence; he received him on the ground floor, the other floors long since destroyed by German shells.

But Marseille was doing more than making a significant financial contribution to rebuilding one of France's war torn northern cities or even putting to rest an old, but not forgotten falsehood. She was demonstrating that just as soldiers from the whole of France had suffered and died together during four long years of unimaginable horror, men and women of the deep, largely protected south empathised with fellow citizens from war-ravaged northern and north-eastern provinces. Whether they hailed from the shattered North or the sun-blessed South they were all part of the Union Sacrée. The Place de Marseille in Arras and the Boulevard d'Arras in Marseille would stand forever as proof of their towns' co-sanguinity.

Captain Piper's New Chief

Almost coincident with Régina's trial, a new 'chief' was appointed to the post of Head of SIS Marseiile, one Major Ernan Forbes-Dennis. His wife joined him in Marseille – she pointed out that it took longer for a wife to be cleared by military regulations to join her husband than 'ladies with less formal relationships'! Subsequently Ernan and his (spy) novelist wife Phyllis Bottome founded a school, Tannerhof situated in the Austrian Alps. One pupil named Ian Fleming lapped up stories of the Dennis-Forbes' time in Marseilles, undoubtedly including ones about Agent Régina Diana. Phyllis encouraged the young Fleming to write, eventually becoming his mentor and friend – her biographer and other intelligence historians argue that James Bond is modelled on her own Mark Chalmers, hero of *The Life Line* (1946). In her autobiography, she remembered wartime Marseille being 'an international hide-out for spies who came and went from all directions, usually escaping recognition.'

U-Boat Commander Otto Schultze

In 1936, a year before his retirement Otto Schultze was promoted to full Admiral, being recalled to Active Service in the Second World War. His (and U-63's) record of having sunk fifty-four ships including *Transylvania* and damaged nine others earned him multiple decorations including Prussia's highest military award, Pour le Mérite, for his outstanding leadership and naval planning skills as well as his many successful submarine operations. Following the Armistice, U-boat 63 was surrendered on 16 January 1919 and broken up at Blyth, 1919–20. His son, Heinz-Otto, also a much-decorated U-boat commander, was killed when U-849 was sunk in the South Atlantic in November 1943. Schultze died on 22 January 1966.

HMT *Transylvania*

Ninety-four years after U-boat U-63 found its target, the wreck of a ship was detected some three miles off Bergeggi island near Italy's Ligurian coast. Lying at a depth of 630m, a first visual inspection indicated that she was broken in two parts about 100m apart. Although over the years, the Italian police had examined countless witness reports in their attempts to determine *Transylvania*'s final location, this lead looked hopeful.

In early October 2011 with the support of the Carabinieri Gruppo Subacqueo di Genova, using a magnetometer that allowed divers to shape- and size-match the wreck, intricate soundings were taken. Four days later an official announcement was made. *Transylvania* had been located. Despite her whereabouts having finally been ascertained, she has not been raised from the seabed; she is the final resting place of some 275 souls who have no other grave but the sea. The names of these lost British and Commonwealth personnel are remembered on panels at the Commonwealth War Graves Commission (CWGC) Savona Memorial. Eighty-three of *Transylvania*'s casualties lie in Savona Town Cemetery, their graves in the perpetual care of the CWGC. Other casualties remain close to where they were washed ashore, in France, Monaco and even Spain.

Six months after the sighting, in a ceremony attended by divers, the Genoa water police, volunteers, Red Cross nurses, officials from all nations involved in the sinking, and rescue, a wreath bearing the Italian and British colours was dropped into the sea, marking the spot where the long-ago tragedy had occurred. A short YouTube film shows not only images of the stricken transport but also the new life she has spawned. *Transylvania* is now home to rare white coral reefs.

Gendarmes

While their contribution to the catching and interrogation of enemy agents met with widespread approval, the gendarmes' role in wartime France was never easy. During and after the war, men of this 'half civilian, half military' force were subject to significant opprobrium from both sides of the military–civilian divide. Nevertheless, they felt, and current research would concur, that their contribution to national defence had been significant. In terms of espionage, they had been instrumental in apprehending many of the spies which Germany and other belligerents had infiltrated into France. Following the letter of the law, they carried out the task assigned to them and their achievements were a source of pride which now, a century later, are slowly being recognised. Without their surveillance, Régina Diana's story might have had a very different ending.

Louis Decosterd and his daughter

Louis exited the life of his ex-wife as quickly as he had entered it. According to Geneva's 'Contrôle des Habitants', once the marriage ended, he left Geneva for an unknown destination. Having refused any paternal authority regarding his infant daughter, he left Marie-Antoinette as the child's sole provider. After the death of her mother and disappearance of her grandmother, the child may have continued to live in France, almost certainly in the Drome area. All attempts to trace her and any descendants have proved fruitless.

Garagiste Cherix

Little is known about the wartime life of Cherix after Régina's execution. One is left surmising that although he disappeared from the Teutonic intelligence network, he had been substantially paid for services rendered and with money in his pocket, fled to the murk and mist of the Broye area of Switzerland with Payerne once again his centre of activity. The owner of what seems to have been an honest rubber and tyre dealership, he long remained in the shadows into which he had, almost certainly intentionally, melted. In the late 1920s, Fernand Ischi, a 'garagiste' friend from his earlier Payerne days with a long-standing reputation as a petty gangster, introduced him to a Protestant minister, Philippe Lugrin, a charismatic, raging anti-Semite and avid supporter of Hitler and subsequently the Nazi party. With his pro-Germanic allegiance so cruelly disappointed by the outcome of the first conflict, Cherix was eager to see his beloved Germany rise from the ashes of defeat. Willing to do whatever it took to give Germany back her lost honour, Cherix flew like a moth to Hitler, the Nazis and most specifically, Lugrin's flame.

In 1942, the Ischi siblings, accompanied by another thug, hit the headlines by participating in the brutal assassination of Jewish cattle dealer, Arthur Bloch. Cherix's contribution to this ugly business (in which Lugrin was one of the main participants and which is still considered the darkest episode in the 1939–1945 wartime history of the canton of Vaud) was peripheral enough for him to avoid arrest but the police were aware of his political leanings and vicious character. Unfazed by this latest brush with the law, he reappears in the neighbouring town of Corcelles-près-Payerne as owner of the region's first official brothel. Payerne being a garrison town, this latest business venture soon flourished. We will never know if 'pillow talk' from this brothel, like that indulged in by his long-dead mistress Régina Diana, wove its way back to Berlin.

Louise-Jeanne and Joseph Avvico

The last definite sighting of Mme Avvico relates to her dead daughter's effects. On 31 July 1920 Louise-Jeanne wrote to the Prison Governor requesting the return of Marie-Antoinette's belongings including her trunk, linen, clothes and jewellery, which had been held in the Présentines prison since her arrest. On 27 October 1920, in response to what might be termed some 'chivvying' from his chain of command, Commander Martin admits that both Louise-Jeanne's letter and, more puzzlingly, the deceased's effects, are nowhere to be found. As far as he is concerned, the case is closed.

Mystery surrounds the post-war life of Louise-Jeanne. A scribble in the Geneva's Contrôle des Habitants suggests that she too was shot by the French authorities supposedly for her involvement in her daughter's network. But no official document, either French or Swiss, confirms this theory. Perhaps it stemmed from an error in one of the court papers which stated that 'Louise-Jeanne Avvico' had been executed on 5 January 1918 when this clearly relates to Marie-Antoinette. No record of an execution can be found in the Archives Communales de Collonges, her birth town. Not that the *mairie* was particularly helpful or eager to shed light on this conundrum, no trace could be found. A similar question mark also remains over Joseph Avvico. Surprisingly, in the light of his relatively successful business, he seems to have left Geneva in about 1913 never to reappear. Perhaps he returned to his native Pinerolo and became another cog in his daughter's wheel, with his wife joining him in 1920. The Geneva authorities may have been pleased to erase all traces of a family who had alerted the French to the fact that their city, like so much of Switzerland, had harboured a nest of spies.

Epilogue:
A Personal Reflection about Régina Diana

A question we have frequently asked ourselves over the past three years is why we believed the story of Régina Diana, an 'enemy spy', was worth telling. As we, like most of our readers, had been brought up to consider 1914–1918 Germany as 'the foe', considerable mental gymnastics and discarding of prejudices had to occur before we could hope to get close to, empathise with, and understand her world. Although there is much that will remain forever hidden from the researcher relating to her short and chaotic life, we feel it is fitting that she should take her rightful place in the pantheon of female intelligence agents who accepted that their life might count for little when the cause of those for whom they were working was at stake.

Régina Diana, the queen of intelligence hunting, used her talents aptly. Cultivating her skills as a milliner and her powerful singing voice, she lured men to her bed. She provided her masters with information which, like that amassed by Louise de Bettignies and the lionised spies working for the Allied cause, was responsible for the deaths of countless soldiers and, in Régina's case, the sinking of thousands of tons of shipping.

A century after her lonely death, she has emerged from the shadows into which the French authorities tried so hard to thrust her and perhaps were even continuing to so do when we began our investigations at Vincennes in February 2014. For us, she started as a barely-glimpsed figure, one that we could not quite dismiss, constantly dancing on the periphery of our vision. Yet she walked with us for months, a constant little voice at the back of our heads telling us to keep persevering, for her story, like that of so many of the forgotten women of the First World War, was worth telling.

Sir Winston Churchill acknowledged that 'writing a book is an adventure. To begin with it is a toy and an amusement. Then it becomes a mistress, then it becomes a master, then it becomes a tyrant'. Nothing could more aptly sum up our long journey in the company of Régina Diana. Initially, we felt little more than idle curiosity about her, slowly this curiosity turned into both amusement and bemusement, then into an addiction until the addiction became an obsession, an obsession to which our respective spouses will attest! If she is satisfied with our attempts to recreate both her life and the historical background against which she is best understood, may she, in her unknown and lost grave 'somewhere in Marseille', finally rest at peace.

Vivien Newman, England, and David Semeraro, Switzerland, 2016

Select Bibliography

Adams, Jefferson, *Historical Dictionary of German Intelligence* Scarecrow Press, Plymouth 2009

Aguet, Joel, *De La Brasserie De L Espérance au Casino-Théâtre Naissance d'un Lieu de Spectacle à Genève 1880–1914* Conference paper delivered 5 June 2012

Akerman, Nadine, 'Ten Things You Never Knew about Elizabeth Stuart The Winter Queen' *http://blog.oup.com/2015/11/*

Altmann, Dr, *La Psychologie de l'Espion* in Espionnage Contre-Espionnage vol 2

Andrews, J. Cutler, *The South Reports the Civil War* University of Pittsburgh Press, 1995

Antier, Chantal, *Louise de Bettignies Espionne et Heroïne de la grande Guerre* Tallandier 2013

Auberson David, *La Suisse 'Terre Bénie des Espions'* in *Actes du colloque organisé à Nanterre et à Amiens du 8 au 11 décembre 1988, Nanterre 190: Publications de I'Université de Nanterre (hereafter Actes),* pp. 293–306

Audoin-Rouzeau, Stéphane, *'Bourrage de crâne' et information en France en 1914–1918,* in: Becker, Jean-Jacques / Audoin-Rouzeau, Stéphane (eds.): *Les Sociétés européennes et la guerre de 1914–1918.* Actes, pp. 163–174

Berlière, Jean-Marc ed., *Justices Militaires et Guerres Mondiales (Europe 1914–1950* Presses Universitaires de Louvain 2014

Bismarck, Otto Von, *L'Attaché Militaire et le Service des Renseignements* in Lacaze op. cit. Vol. 1

Bottome, Phyllis, *The Goal* Vanguard 1962

Boura, Olivier, *Marseille ou la mauvaise réputation* Arléa Poche 2001

Bradshaw, George, *Bradshaw's Continental Railway Guide: For Travellers Through Europe, with an Epitomized Description of Each Country, and Maps of Europe, Showing the Lines of Railways Opened* 1913 edition

Brouri, Malik, *Saisons de guerre ou Journal d'un conscrit colonial en 1917* Baudelaire 2013

Buffet, Eugénie, *Ma Vie Mes Amours, Mes Aventures* pdf. accessed via www.dutempsdescerisesauxfeuillesmortes.net

Buzzi, Pierre Louis, *La prostitution à Toul pendant la Grande Guerre* in *Etudes Touloises 2014, 149* pp. 15-18

Camous, Claude, *La Grande Guerre à Marseille* Autres Temps, 2013

Chessex, Jacques, *Un Juif pour l'exemple* Grasset & Fasquelle, 2009

Cheyronnaud Jacques, *Marseille et «son» Alcazar. Les termes d'une doxa*

Conference paper delivered 16 January 2012 (lehall.com)

Cohen, Robin, *The Cambridge Survey of World Migration,* Cambridge University Press, 1995 (2010)

Conway, Kelley, *Chanteuse in the City: The Realist Singer in French Film* University of California Press 2004

Delord, Dominique, Université d'automne du patrimoine de la chanson – « Marseille- Cité de la musique. La chanson entre histoire, paroles et musique » sourced via docplayer.fr

Du Bois, Pierre, *Le Mal Suisse Pendant la Première Guerre Mondiale: Fragments d'un discours sur les relations entre Alémaniques, Romands et Tessinois au début du vingtième siècle in Revue européenne des sciences sociales T. 18 No. 53 1980 pp. 43-66*

Easton, Laird ed., *Journey to the Abyss: The Diaries of Count Harry Kessler, 1880–1918* Random House 2013

Echinard, Pierre., *L'espace du spectacle à Marseille, deux siècles d'évolution.* In: *Méditerranée, tome 73, 2–3-1991. Marseille et l'aire métropolitaine hier et aujourd'hui.* pp. 39–46

Fanet, Fabrice, *Les Militaires qui ont changé la France* Cherche- Midi 2008

Faure, Claude, *Aux Services de la République: du BCRA à la DGSE* Fayard, 2004

Fell, Hans W., *L'Exploitation des Renseignements d'agents et ses Résultats* in Lacaze op. cit vol. 1

La Route qui conduit à l'ennemi ou l'espionnage à travers les pays neutres in Lacaze, op. cit vol. 1

Fulcher, Jane ed., *The Oxford Handbook of the New Cultural History of Music* "Yvette Guilbert and the Re-evaluation of the *Chanson Populaire*" OUP 2011

Gex, Nicolas, *Louis Dumur ou un regard critique sur la Suisse durant la première guerre mondiale* in ed. Vuilleumier *La Suisse et la Guerre de 1914–1918*

Goldstein, Robert Justin, *The Frightful Stage: Political Censorship of the Theater in Nineteenth Century Europe* Berghahn Books, Oxford 2009.

Graves, Armgaard Kirk, *The Secrets of the German War Office* A. L. Burt, New York nd.

Guilbert, Yvette, *The Song of My Life: Memories* Harrap, 1929

Heiniger, Alix and Thomas, David, *Mobility and Social Control: French Immigration in Geneva during the Belle Epoque* in ed. Panter Sarah

Hieber, Hanne, *Mademoiselle Docteur: The Life and Service of Imperial Germany's Only Female Intelligence Officer, Journal of Intelligence History*, 5:2, 91–108 fn.3 2005

Hiley, Nicholas, *Internal security in wartime: The rise and fall of P.M.S.2, 1915–1917, Intelligence and National Security*, 1:3, 395–415, 1986. DOI: 10.1080/02684528608431864

Hochsfield Adam, *To End All Wars: How the First World War Divided Britain 1914–1918*

Inglin, Meinrad, *La Suisse dans un miroir* Editions de l'Aire 2013 (trans from German by Michel Mamboury)

Jardine, Lisa, BBC A Point of View 24/02/2013 http://www.bbc.co.uk/news/magazine-21532311

Joseph, Mathilde, *Le Poilu de Music-hall. L'image du poilu dans les music-halls parisiens pendant la grande guerre* in Guerres Mondiales et Conflits Contemporains no. 197 Mars 2000

Kipling, Rudyard, *The Complete Verse* Kyle Cathié, 1990

Krakovitch, Odile, *La Censure des théâtres durant la grande guerre* quoted by Mathilde Joseph

Labarre, Léon, *L'Espionnage Boche en Suisse 138* 1919

Lacaze, L. (translator), *L'espionnage et le contre-espionnage pendant la guerre mondiale d'après les archives militaires du Reich.* Nouveau Monde editions, Paris 2013 Vols 1 & 2

Langendorf, Jean-Jacques, *Le Desarroi et L'Effort: L'Armée Suisse 1914–1918* in ed. Vuilleumier

Lanoir, Paul, *L'Espionnage Allemand en France: Son Organisation – Ses Dangers – Les Remèdes Nécessaires* Cocuaud, 1908

Le Naour Jean-Yves, *Marseille 1914–1918* Gaussen 2014, pp. 405–427

Leu, Stéphane, *Passer la Frontière en temps de guerre: Hommes et Marchandises. L'exemple de la Frontière Franco-Suisse* in ed. Vuilleumier *Actes*

Likosky, Stephan, *Filles de Joie: French Prostitution on the Early Postcard http://www.metropostcard.com/metropcbloga11.html*

Luc, Jean-Noel, *Gendarmerie, état et société au XIXe siècle* Sorbonne 2002

Mackaman, Douglas and Mays, Michael (eds.), *World War I and the Cultures of Modernity* University Press of Mississippi 2000

Maddison, Angus, *Development Centre Studies The World Economy Historical Statistics* OECD, 2003

Magill, Frank ed., *The 20th Century A-GI: Dictionary of World Biography Vol. 7 Routledge*

Martin, Thomas, *Empires of Intelligence: Security Services and Colonial Disorder after 1914* University of California Press, 2007

Mason, Laura, *Singing the French Revolution Popular Culture and Politics, 1787–1799* Cornell University Press, 1996

Massard, Emile, *Les Espionnes à Paris* Albin Michel, Paris 1922

Meuwly, Olivier, *De L'Union Sacrée à la Guerre Ouverte : Les Partis politiques en Suisse entre 1914–1918* in ed. Vuilleumier *Actes*, pp. 177–205

Michel, Albert, *Manuel pratique de Police. Matières enseignées aux Centres d'instruction pour Alsaciens et Lorrains élèves gendarmes*

Miller, Paul B., *From Revolutionaries to Citizens* Duke University Press, 2002

Mistinguett, *Mistinguett, Queen of the Paris Night*. Trans Lucienne Hill. Elek 1954

Morgan, Janet, *The Secrets of Rue St Roch* Penguin, 2004

Ostrymiecz Urbanski, A., *Le Contole Postale* in Lacaze op. cit. vol. 1

Panel, Louis, *Gendarmerie et Contre-Espionnage 1914–1918* La Documentation Française, 2004

Panel, Louis, *Espionnage et trahison Les agents de renseignements condamnés par des conseils de guerre français pendant la Première Guerre mondiale in* Berlière op.cit

Panel, Louis, *La Grande Guerre des Gendarmes: Forcer, au besoin, leur obéissance'?: la Gendarmerie nationale et la Grande Guerre des Français (1914–1918)* Nouveau Monde, 2013

Panter, Sarah ed., *Mobility and Biography* de Gruyter Oldenbourg, 2016 (ebook version)

Pöhlmann Markus, 'German Intelligence at War, 1914–1918' *Journal of Intelligence History* 2005 also in Wiebes op.cit

Ray, Oscar, *Histoire de L'espionnage* Gallimard, Paris 1936

Rearick, Charles, *The French in Love and War: Popular Culture in the Era of the World Wars*, Yale University Press, 1997

Roegels Fritz-Karl, *La Censure était-elle nécessaire ?* in Lacaze Vol. 1

Simon-Carrère Anne, *Chanter La Grande Guerre* Champ Vallon Lonrai, 2013

Sorrie, Charles, Censorship of the Press in France 1917–1918 sourced via etheses.lse.ac.uk/3110/1/Sorrie_Censorship_of_the_Press_in_France.pdf

Steinberg Jonathan, *Why Switzerland?* Cambridge University Press, 1996

Sweeney, Régina, *Singing our Way to Victory French Cultural Politics and Music During the Great War* Wesleyan University Press 2001 see also Mackamann et al

Sylvie, Clair, *14–18, Marseille Dans la Grande Guerre* Bizalion, 2014

Thébaud Françoise, *La Femme au temps de la Guerre de 14* Stock/Laurence Pernoud, 1994

Thilo, Emile, *La repression de l'espionnage militaire* Revue Militaire Suisse 81 1936 p. 592

Thomson, Basil, *Queer People* Hodder & Stoughton, 1922

Three Village Historical Society, *A Case for Anna Smith Strong: Her Relationship with the Setauket-Based Culper Spy Ring,* 2014

Todd, Janet, *Aphra Behn Studies* Cambridge University Press, 1996

Tu, Hsuan-Yung, *The Pursuit of God's Glory: Francis Walsingham's Espionage In Elizabethan Politics, 1568–1588* (PhD thesis 2012 University of York)

Tuchmann, Barbara, *The Guns of August* Ballantine Books, 2004 (1962)

Valode Philippe, *Espions et Espionnes de la Grande Guerre* First Histoire, 2014

Vidal-Naquet, Clémentine ed., *Correspondances Conjugales 1914–1918 : Dans l'intimité de la grande guerre* Robert Lafont, 2014 (Letter from Abel Ferry to his wife 3 September 1914)

Vuilleumier Christophe, *Les Suisses dans les armées étrangères* in *Actes*, pp. 479–493

Vuilleumier Christophe, *La Lutte Contre l'espionnage en Suisse pendant la première guerre mondiale* in *Guerres Mondiales et Conflits Contemporains* 253, (2014/1) Paris pp. 73–88

Vuilleumier Christophe, *L'espionnage en Suisse pendant la première guerre mondiale* Revue Administrative 397 and 398 Paris (2014) pp. 9–18 and 119–130

Vuilleumier Christophe, *La Suisse face à l'espionnage 1914–1918* Slatkine 2015

Vuilleumier Christophe ed., *La Suisse et La Guerre de 1914–1918 Actes du colloque du 10 au 12 septembre 2014 au Château de Penthes* Slatkine Geneva 2015

Warfusel, Bertrand, *Le Secret de la défense nationale* PhD thesis Paris, 1994

Watkins, Glenn, *Proof through the Night: Music and the Great War* University of California Press, 2003

West, Nigel, *Historical Dictionary of World War One Intelligence* Rowman & Littlefield, Plymouth 2014

Wiebes, Cees, *Intelligence and the War in Bosnia 1992–1995 (Studies in Intelligence History)* James Bennett Pty, 2003

Winter, J. M., *The Experience of War* Greenwich 2000

Wood, Eric Fisher, 'A Dispatch Bearer in the Diplomatic Service' in *True Stories of World War 1, Complete: The World War: Blood and Tears of Thirty Million Soldiers* VM eBooks, 2016

Ziegler, Jean, *Une Suisse au-dessus de toute soupçon* Editions du Seuil, 1976

English texts published London, French texts published Paris unless otherwise stated

Websites (all accessed between April and September 2016)

www.1914–1918.ch

www.1914–1918.invisionzone.com (Lieutenant Philip Murphy)

http://www.24heures.ch/vaud-regions/1943-Le-proces-des-nazis-d-ici/story/18971159

www.abelard.org/france/dating_postcards.php 6

www.arcmanor.com/FDL/AofW5674.pdf p.201 (for Henri Jomini, trans 1862 G.H.Mendell and W. P Craighill).

www.americancivilwarstory.com/elizabeth-van-lew.html

www.ampisolabergeggi.it/it/news/64-transylvania.html

www.azionemare.org (*SS Transylvania*)

www.britishnewspaperarchive.co.uk

www.civilwarsaga.com/rose-oneal-greenhow

www.cheminsdememoire.gouv.fr/en/les-marraines-de-guerre

www.chemistry.about.com

www.dar.org Daughters of the American Revolution

www.decouvrir-marseille.marseille.fr/histoire-de-marseille

www.elizabethwalne.co.uk/blog/2014/1/31/i-hope-it-wont-be-so-exciting-as-this-sister-haywards-great.html (Jessica Hayward)

www.encyclopedia.1914–1918-online.net/article/espionage

www.forums.qrz.com/index.php?threads/memorial-day-of-british-s-s-transylvania-torpedoed-in-front-of-the-isle-of-bergeggi.349751/

www.france-pub.com/world-war-1.php (for French battle statistics)

www.goodreads.com (Churchill quote)

www.grehcognin.fr/images/deux_mille/marraines-reduites.pdf

www.gutenberg.org/files/1946/1946-h/1946-h.htm) Carl von Clausewitz

www.hebdo.ch/hebdo/mieux-comprendre/detail/1914–1918-grande-guerre-suisse (Mis en ligne le 19.12.2013 à 05:58)

www.hls-dhs-dss.ch (dictionnaire historique de la Suisse)

www.hrp.org.uk/tower-of-london/history-and-stories/tower-of-london-remembers/the-tower-during-the-war/prison-and-place-of-execution/

www.hutchinscenter.fas.harvard.edu/bowser-mary-elizabeth-1839-union-spy-during-civil-war

www.irishbrigade.eu /other-men/germans/nicholai-deptIIIb/nicholai.html

www.library.leeds.ac.uk/features/349/article/72/aphra_behn _the_unpaid_spy

www.memoiredeshommes.sga.defense.gouv.fr

www.metropostcard.com/metropcbloga11.html

www.militariahelvetica.ch

www.musee-histoire-marseille-voie-historique.fr

www.nationalmuseum.ch

www.ncmuseumofhistory.org

www.newspapers.com

www.opinionator.blogs.nytimes.com/2012/06/21/a-black-spy-in-the-confederate-white-house/?_r=0 (Mary Bowser)

www.paperlessarchive.com (Civil War: Confederate Spy – Rose O'Neal Greenhow: Papers – Letters – Memoirs – Histories)

www.police-nationale.interieur.gouv.fr/Organisation/Direction-Centrale-de-la-Police-Judiciaire/Histoire-de-la-police-judiciaire

www. recherche.ge.ch

www.routard.com/guide/marseille/1815/histoire.html

www.scarletfinders.co.uk/64.html (Maude McCarthy's diaries transcribed by Sue Light)

www.sites.lafayette.edu/specialcollections/2013/06/10/our-alsace-lorraine-picture-postcard-collection/

www.smithsonianmag.com/ist/?next=/history/elizabeth-van-lew-an-unlikely-union-spy-158755584/

www.spymuseumberlin.com

www.suntzusaid.com

www.swissinfo.ch/eng/congress-of-vienna_the-day-switzerland-became-neutral/41335520 (Pauchard, Olivier: The Day Switzerland Became Neutral)

www.switzerland1914–1918.net/blog/kilometre-zero-where-the-western-front-met-the-swiss-frontier

www.tdg.ch « Une Genevoise fusillée en 1918 pour espionnage de guerre » 1 March 2015

www.trove.nla.gov.au/newspaper/result?q=Regina+Diane (all Australian newspapers accessed via this site)

www.uboat.net/wwi/men/commanders/313.html ('Deadly Mediterranean')
www.universalis.fr/encyclopedie/paul-deroulede
www.wikipedia.org
www.wrecksite.eu/wreck.aspx?37314
www.youtube.com/watch?v=MUsuuDNmcZM (images of *Transylvania* today)
https://www.youtube.com/watch?v=POicrexHnhQ (Les Espions, C'est pas Sorcier, France3 Television Program)
www.zinfos974.com/Juliette-Dodu-Heroine-controversee_a7202.html

Archives:
Imperial War Museum

IWM PP/MCR/120 Sir Vernon Kell Reel 1SVK/2 Security Intelligence in War p.128
Kirke, Walter Diaries Imperial War Museum Department of Documents
Sound recording for Sergeant Williams http://www.iwm.org.uk/collections/item/object/80009538

Peter Liddle

LIDDLE/WW1/WO/009 Nursing Sister Burgess (Diary transcript)

Service Historique de la Défense (Vincennes, Paris)

SHAT 9N978 (Anzoulay)

Historial Péronne

Fonds Capitaine Vanheeckhoet

Switzerland

Archives Cantonales, Contrôle des habitants de la République et canton de Genève, Ville de Genève
Archives Communales, Petit-Saconnex, République et canton de Genève.
Archives Cantonales, Contrôle des habitants du Canton de Vaud, Lausanne
Archives Communales, Payerne, Canton de Vaud.

France

Registre National des Matricules Militaires, Paris
Archives Nationales d'outre-mer, Paris

Files on Marie-Antoinette Avvico alias Régina Diana accessed via:

http://www.memoiredeshommes.sga.defense.gouv.fr/ specifically: archives_SHDGR_GR_10_J_1721_12_28898_001 to 0480 with pages 0071–0072 covering the automatic appeal

Newspapers

Daily Mirror 22 September 1917; 8 January 1918
Le Figaro 20 – 30 August 1914
Gazette de Lausanne 1 August 1914–31 December 1918
Journal de Genève 1 August 1914–31 December 1918
Le Petit Marseillais August – September 1914
Le Petit Provençal 30 August 1914
Le Sémaphore (Marseille) August – September 1914
Philadelphia Press 19 January 1862, 5 February 1862
The Semi-Weekly State Journal Raleigh, North Carolina 7 June 1862
The Sun (New York), April 07, 1918, Section 5 Magazine Section, Page 10, Image 58
Sunday Mirror 10 June 1917 (HMT *Transylvania*)
The Times 18 December 1919
War Illustrated 17 November 1917; 2 February 1918

Index